THE HISTORY OF THE NEW WORLD

THE HISTORY OF THE NEW WORLD

Girolamo Benzoni's *Historia del Mondo Nuovo*

Edited by Robert C. Schwaller and Jana Byars
Translated by Jana Byars

The Pennsylvania State University Press
University Park, Pennsylvania

Library of Congress Cataloging-in-Publication Data

Names: Benzoni, Girolamo, 1519– , author. | Byars,
Jana, translator, editor. | Schwaller, Robert C.,
1981– , editor.
Title: The history of the New World : Benzoni's His-
toria del mondo nuovo / Girolamo Benzoni ; translated by Jana Byars ; edited by Robert C. Schwaller
and Jana Byars.
Other titles: Historia del mondo nuovo. English |
Latin American originals.
Description: University Park, Pennsylvania :
The Pennsylvania State University Press, [2017] |
Series: Latin American originals | Includes biblio-
graphical references and index.
Summary: "An abridged, annotated translation of
Girolamo Benzoni's 1572 History of the New
World, which describes firsthand encounters
between Europeans and Native Americans, New
World geography, and indigenous flora and
fauna"—Provided by publisher.
Identifiers: LCCN 2016031047 | ISBN 9780271077574
(pbk. : alk. paper)
Subjects: LCSH: America—Early accounts to 1600. |
Latin America—History—To 1600.
Classification: LCC E141 .B4213 2017 | DDC
970.01—dc23
LC record available at https://lccn.loc.gov/2016031047

The Pennsylvania State University Press is a member
of the Association of American University Presses.

It is the policy of The Pennsylvania State University
Press to use acid-free paper. Publications on uncoated
stock satisfy the minimum requirements of Ameri-
can National Standard for Information Sciences—
Permanence of Paper for Printed Library Material,
ANSI Z39.48–1992.

CONTENTS

ILLUSTRATIONS

Latin American Originals (LAO) is a series of primary source texts on colonial Latin America. LAO volumes are accessible, affordable editions of texts translated into English—most of them for the very first time. Of the eleven volumes now in print, eight illuminate aspects of the Spanish invasions in the Americas during the long century of 1494–1614, and three push our understandings of the spiritual conquest into surprising new territories.

Taken in the chronological order of their primary texts, *Of Cannibals and Kings* (LAO 7) comes first. It presents the earliest written attempts to describe Native American cultures, offering striking insight into how the first Europeans in the Americas struggled from the very start to conceive a New World. *The Native Conquistador* (LAO 10) comes next, telling the story of the famous Spanish conquest expeditions into Mexico and Central America from 1519 to 1524—but through an indigenous perspective, built around an alternative leading protagonist (Ixtlilxochitl, the king of Tetzcoco), written by his great-great-grandson. Viewed through the prism of the Ixtlilxochitl dynasty, the so-called Conquest of Mexico looks startlingly different.

Next, chronologically, are LAO 2, 1, and 9. *Invading Guatemala* shows how reading multiple accounts of conquest wars (in this case, Spanish, Nahua, and Maya versions of the Guatemalan conflict of the 1520s) can explode established narratives and suggest a more complex and revealing conquest story. *Invading Colombia* challenges us to view the difficult Spanish invasion of Colombia in the 1530s as more representative of conquest campaigns than the better-known assaults on the Aztec and Inca empires. It complements *The Improbable Conquest*, which presents letters written between 1537 and 1556 by Spaniards struggling to found a colony along the hopefully named Río de la Plata. Their trials and tribulations make the persistence of the colonists seem improbable indeed.

This newest addition to the series, *The History of the New World* (LAO 11), slots in next. It offers the first English translation since 1847 of significant portions of a book that was first published in Venice in 1565 and went on to be a sixteenth-century best seller in five languages. Its success matters in part because its author, the Italian merchant-adventurer Girolamo Benzoni, mixed sharp observations and sympathy for indigenous peoples with imaginary tales and wild history, influencing generations of early modern readers and challenging modern readers to sort out fact from fable.

The Conquest on Trial (LAO 3) features a fictional indigenous embassy filing a complaint over the conquest in a court in Spain—the Court of Death. That text, the first theatrical examination of the conquest published in Spain, effectively condensed contemporary debates on colonization into one dramatic package. It contrasts well with *Defending the Conquest* (LAO 4), which presents a spirited, ill-humored, and polemic apologia for the Spanish Conquest, written in 1613 by a lesser-known veteran conquistador.

LAO volumes 5, 6, and 8 all explore aspects of Spanish efforts to implant Christianity in the New World. *Gods of the Andes* presents the first English edition of a 1594 manuscript describing Inca religion and the campaign to convert native Andeans. Its Jesuit author is surprisingly sympathetic to pre-conquest beliefs and practices, viewing them as preparing Andeans for the arrival of the faith from Spain. *Forgotten Franciscans* casts new light on the spiritual conquest and the conflictive cultural world of the Inquisition in sixteenth-century Mexico. Both LAO 5 and 6 expose wildly divergent views within the church in Spanish America—both on native religions and on how to replace them with Christianity. Complementing those two volumes by revealing the indigenous side to the same process, *Translated Christianities* presents religious texts translated from Nahuatl and Yucatec Maya. Designed to proselytize and ensure the piety of indigenous parishioners, these texts show how such efforts actually contributed to the development of local Christianities, leading to fascinatingly multifaceted outcomes.

The source texts in LAO volumes are colonial-era rare books or archival documents, written in indigenous languages such Nahuatl and Maya, or in European languages, to which list this volume now adds Italian. LAO contributing authors are historians, anthropologists, and scholars of literature; they have developed a specialized knowledge that allows them to locate, translate, and present these texts in a way that contributes to scholars' understanding of the period, while also making them readable for students and nonspecialists. Robert Schwaller and Jana Byars are scholars of this ilk, allowing them to create this fascinating and important contribution to the series.

—Matthew Restall

ACKNOWLEDGMENTS

This short volume owes its existence to the Department of History at the Pennsylvania State University. Just as the strange territory of New Spain and the characters he met there inspired Benzoni, so, too, did the Weaver Building and its inhabitants inspire us. Latin Americanists and early modern Europeanists frequently found themselves huddled together in the drafty halls of the Weaver Building, in the same seminars and working with the same faculty members. We read one another's work and cheered one another on through papers, comps, and dissertations. Thanks to these shared experiences, when Jana ran across an early edition of Benzoni's *Historia del Mondo Nuovo* at the Newberry Library, it only made sense that she would contact Rob, and that the two of us would work together to bring this volume to life. We would like to express our appreciation to the other institutions that have helped us along the way: the departments of history at Iowa State University and the University of Kansas, the Newberry Library, and the Gale Family Library at the Minnesota History Center. Eleanor Goodman, at Penn State University Press, and Matthew Restall, the series editor, offered help and encouragement throughout the process, from our first contact until the ink dried on the contract. We are grateful for the two anonymous reviewers who helped us better envision the significance of Benzoni's work and this edition. We thank the Jayhawks and Cyclones who read earlier versions of this project, and Janelle Fox and Rachel Schwaller for helping to clarify points of translation and gaps in annotation. We are thankful for the enduring support of our friends and families, particularly as it became clear that this quick little side project was neither quick nor little.

Introduction

"Being young, only twenty-two, and desiring to see the world like many others, and having heard word of the new countries just discovered in the Indies many call the New World, I determined to go." In his opening sentence, Girolamo Benzoni explains to his audience exactly why he braved a transatlantic crossing in 1541. Like many of his contemporaries, he sought adventure. He definitely found it, traversing breathtaking surroundings, encountering tattooed and pierced natives, engaging in deadly battles, and barely surviving almost continual hardship. More than once, Benzoni found himself at death's door yet managed to escape with his life. Although his travels are presented as an adventure tale, he had a less glamorous motive for traveling across the globe: Benzoni was a merchant. In his travels throughout the Americas, he pursued various trade ventures. It is difficult to judge just how successful he was at finding his riches. He omits most of his business dealings; only rarely does he provide details on the price of wine or gold. He certainly asserts his prosperity, telling his readers that he made a fortune and was ready to bring a load of gold back to Milan. Like other early travelers, Benzoni became an amateur naturalist. He recorded detailed descriptions of indigenous flora and fauna, almost always oddly colored by the pressing pains of hunger or thirst. At the same time, his writings engage in explicit political commentary. Although a traveler in Spanish America, he despised the Spanish. At almost every turn, Benzoni criticizes Spanish methods of conquest and governance, while frequently siding with Native Americans.

More than a decade after he initially departed northern Italy for parts unknown, he found himself expelled from the overseas kingdoms of Spain. He packed his thousands of ducats and left, set to retrace his steps to Europe. Unfortunately, he suffered shipwreck and inclement weather before he got far. He had to stay in Havana for several miserable months waiting for a vessel strong enough, and weather good enough, to carry him home. He ultimately arrived in Spain in 1556, penniless, exhausted, and full of stories. With nothing left to peddle but his memories, he decided to write them down in his *History of the New World*. Originally published in 1565, Benzoni's history quickly captured the attention of readers across Europe.

Benzoni's narrative contributed to a growing corpus of travel narratives that related the explorations and adventures of Europeans as they traveled to parts unknown.[1] His work was very well received for several reasons: he included harrowing stories, he offered descriptions of the indigenous animals and plants that Europeans had never even imagined, and he described a completely new group of people and beliefs. Just as Spain's continental ascendency seemed unstoppable, Benzoni offered a vitriolic description of the barbarity of the Spanish that brought their moral authority to rule and exploit the New World into question. The mix of adventure, exotic people and places, and anti-Spanish diatribe made *The History of the New World* an immediate best seller. Benzoni's narrative provides a unique firsthand account of the Spanish conquest by an Italian. Its anti-Spanish rhetoric represents an understudied but historically significant contribution to the Black Legend of Spanish colonialism. As a whole, *The History of the New World* provides readers with a rich ethnographic text that offered its early modern readers a tantalizing blend of travelogue, adventure tale, and anti-Spanish propaganda.

Benzoni and the Early Modern Travel Narrative

Most of the very little we know for certain about Benzoni comes from his first line: he left for the Indies in 1541, when he was twenty-two.

1. In the early fourteenth century, the *Travels of Marco Polo* enthralled European audiences with its glimpses of the Far East. During Benzoni's youth, letters written by Hernán Cortés were published almost immediately after reaching Spain and became instant best sellers. See Cortés, *Cartas de relación*.

Other clues come from his two dedications. The second (and shorter) dedication was written in 1572, so we know that he was still alive at that point. In the first, written in 1565, Benzoni tells Pope Paul IV that he is the child of a "humble father," from a "house gone to ruin, in part because of the continuing war, and just as much because fortune has always been [his family's] enemy."[2] Because his father could not support him at university, he instead sent Benzoni throughout Europe, to "various provinces: France, Spain, Germany, and the other cities in Italy."[3] It was in these distant cities that he first heard of the wonders of the New World and developed an "extreme desire" to go. Though he never again speaks directly of his upbringing, the narrative supports his claim to be a down-on-his-luck merchant and curious traveler.

Benzoni's book has a longer and better-documented pedigree. *La historia del Mondo Nuovo* was first published in Venice in 1565; it was reissued in 1572 with some minor changes.[4] Far more copies of this second edition are extant, suggesting a larger run. The book was translated and republished quickly. Urban Chauveton translated it into Latin; this edition was published in Geneva by Eustathium Vignon in 1578. The same team issued a French translation in 1579. Nicholas Höniger, a German, translated the work into German from Chauveton's Latin; it was published in Basel in 1579. Benzoni was translated into Dutch in 1610. Europeans were able to read about a dozen more translations and editions by the end of the sixteenth century, and quite a few more in the early seventeenth.[5] There were thirty-two editions in all.[6] The book languished for about a century, until the appearance of a new French translation in 1835. Unsurprisingly, Benzoni's hispanophobic text was translated into Spanish only in 1967, and even then only in the colonies, in Caracas, Venezuela. It was not published in Spain proper until 1989.[7]

2. "Onde essendo io nato di humil padre nella mirabil Città di Milano, & essendo andata la nostra casa piu volte in sinistro, & rovina: tanto per le continue guerre, quanto per altri accidenti della iniqua fortuna sempre nimica nostra." Benzoni, *Historia del Mondo Nuovo* (1565), iii.

3. "Non potendo il padre mio allo studio sustenarmi, mi mandò di età giovanile in varie Provincie, Francia, Ispagna, Alemagna, & altre città d'Italia." Ibid.

4. A complete list of early editions of Benzoni's text can be found in the bibliography.

5. Caraci, *Scopritori e viaggiatori*, 41.

6. Jones, "Ethnographer's Sketch," 144.

7. The Italians kept track of Benzoni, in whom their interest never waned. His narrative was republished in Italian, again in Venice, in 1575 in its entirety. It was also

Anglophones had access to a bit of Benzoni from the early seventeenth century on. The English cleric Samuel Purchas translated and edited a collection of travel narratives by "Englishmen and others" in 1625.[8] He included six pages from Benzoni, whom he called "Jerome Benzos," in his fourth volume. None of Benzoni's book was rendered into English again until the mid-nineteenth century, when the Hakluyt Society—a group founded in 1846 in London to further the study of exploration—published it in its entirety in 1857. The "entirety" is part of why we have chosen to issue this new translation and edition. At its best, Benzoni's account captures the reader's imagination with its rich first-person details and unique perspective. At other times, Benzoni copies other authors almost word for word, passing on specious information with nary a comment. Moreover, the 1857 translation, though serviceable, is clunky and more than a little dated. The current edition contains material written only by Benzoni himself; from the whole text we have skimmed much of the chaff.

Europeans had always loved stories offering adventure in faraway lands and novel, often "monstrous," people.[9] The Greeks told a tale of Hercules stealing the belt of Hippolyte, the Amazon queen, in a distant land. In the Middle Ages, Europeans voraciously consumed the stories of Marco Polo, Odoric of Pordenone, and Sir John Mandeville, with little thought for veracity or even verisimilitude. Rather, the more amazing or awe-inspiring, the better, even if the descriptions were inexact and difficult.[10] Stephen Greenblatt likens the European response to the New World to the "startle reflex" in infants: "eyes widened, arms outstretched, breathing stilled, the whole body momentarily convulsed."[11] Europeans reached for the Western Hemisphere, with its endless jungles, enormous mountains, and strange people unlike anyone ever encountered. Yet that startled moment also contained a flash of panic. This wonder, as Greenblatt characterizes it, involved not only a desire to possess and understand

included in other editions with the work of fellow Italian explorers Antonio Pigafetta and Christopher Columbus in the nineteenth century. Finally, a couple of modern editions remain ubiquitous throughout Italy and are included in the bibliography.

8. See Purchas, *Hakluyts Posthumus or Purchas his Pilgrimes.*

9. See Payne, "From the 'History of Travayle'"; Hadfield, *Amazons, Savages, and Machiavels.*

10. Campbell, *Witness and the Other World*, 223.

11. Greenblatt, *Marvelous Possessions*, 14.

but also more than a hint of terror and horror. Naked cannibals, monstrous beasts, entire societies existed outside of God's plan, and they were dreadful as well as captivating. And so Benzoni's narrative arrived at just the right time. Europeans were in the first throes of New World fever. They consumed more travel literature than ever before and panted over tales of adventure from those recently returned from strange new lands.[12]

The travel literature of the early modern period helped to explain to Europeans not only the newly discovered territories but also how the Old World fit into a new global paradigm. As Claude Lévi-Strauss wrote in his memoir *Tristes tropiques*, "Every landscape appears first of all as a vast chaos, which leaves one free to choose the meaning one wants to give it."[13] Explorers arrived in the New World with a cultural paradigm that they imposed upon the world they found. They understood their world within that framework and transmitted it to their readers. Practically speaking, unique animals were likened to familiar beasts of burden. But beyond that, Europeans rendered the utterly unknown into something culturally identifiable. For instance, Hakluyt rendered naked Indians in the New World as the ancient Picts in imagery. This gave contemporary Europeans a ready category—"savage"—and a narrative for growth: barbarians from Europe became the entirely civilized British Empire. These naked Indians could also become delightful Christian citizens.[14]

Benzoni certainly makes use of this schema. He accentuates the savagery in the Americas, be it via an exhausting passage on bloodthirsty mites capable of crippling a grown man overnight, or magniloquent descriptions of genuine man-eating Indians. He sets up a very clear asymmetrical dichotomy between the indigenous and the Europeans, with religion as his first line of demarcation: superior European Christian opposite inferior pagan indigenous. Benzoni occasionally refers to the indigenous as "brute beasts" in his narration of their senseless pagan rituals, their willingness to murder their children, and their horrifying habit of consuming their neighbors. But he often presents these atrocities in concert with the even greater horrors perpetrated by the Spaniards. The Indians kill their children

12. Whitehead, "South America/Amazonia," 122; Whitfield, *Travel: A Literary History*, chap. 2.

13. Lévi-Strauss, *Tristes tropiques*, 42.

14. Mancall, "Age of Discovery," 41.

in abominable ways, but only to save them from greater abuses at the hands of the Spaniards. Yet there were clear distinctions even within the ranks of the Christians, and Benzoni wants to emphasize them. For Benzoni, and his contemporaries, the Spaniards and Italians represented two different peoples endowed with different moral and cultural characteristics. Benzoni often writes of Spanish foolishness, yet he rarely compares Spaniards and Italians directly.[15] Instead, he makes his anti-Spaniard point by contrasting his fellow Christians with the indigenous. The indigenous may be cannibals, but they are generous when compared to the Spaniards. The Spaniards appear not only as vicious monsters but also as very bad Christians.

The Spanish Empire and the Black Legend

Benzoni's hatred of Spaniards was not unreasonable. Spain was arguably the most powerful country in Europe during the years Benzoni spent tramping through the Americas, and its power was bolstered and maintained by the copious riches of the New World.[16] The marriage of Ferdinand of Aragon and Isabel of Castile in 1469 set the stage for the unification of Spain.[17] In 1492, the end of the Reconquista and the expulsion of the Jews and Muslims furthered their nationalist project. The couple wisely negotiated strategic marriages for their children, most notably pairing their daughter Juana with the Habsburg Philip the Handsome, son of the Holy Roman Emperor. Philip and Juana gave birth to a son, Charles, who became king of Castile and Aragon in 1516, and would be the first monarch to rule those territories with the title king of Spain. The initial union of Castile and Aragon probably did not worry other European kingdoms. In 1520, however, Charles succeeded his grandfather Maximilian and became Charles V, the Holy Roman Emperor and archduke of Austria. Such a confluence of dynastic providence was certainly cause for alarm.

By the 1520s, Charles controlled huge chunks of Europe, including the Netherlands, Austria, Hungary, and much of northern Italy,

15. Enders and Fraser, "Italian in the New World," 22–25.
16. Davis, *Rise of the Atlantic Economies*, chap. 3; Fisher, *Economic Aspects of Spanish Imperialism*, 56–59.
17. For a full treatment of Spain during this time, see Kamen, *Spain, 1469–1714*.

as well as territories in the New World. After inheriting such vast estates, Charles spent most of his life defending them from his rivals. In Italy, Charles would spend thirty years fending off French invasions and internal Italian challenges.[18] As Holy Roman Emperor, he struggled to contain the outbreak of the Protestant Reformation and the vicious warfare it unleashed. In the Americas, French and English pirates threatened his colonists and his treasury.[19] Even the expanding Ottoman Empire encroached on his Austrian possessions. In 1554, Charles chose to retire to a monastery, bequeathing the Holy Roman Empire to his brother, Ferdinand, and leaving Spain, and its empire, to his son, Philip II, who remained embroiled in conflict throughout the sixteenth century.

Benzoni's personal experience with this history came through a set of these conflicts called the Italian Wars. Waged between 1494 and 1559, these wars involved most of the major European kingdoms, as they each vied for power over the Italian Peninsula. Benzoni's home, the Duchy of Milan, was constantly at war during this period. Although the Milanese could have developed a grudge against many foreign interlopers, including the papacy, the French, the Florentines, the Ottomans, and the Venetians, among others, the Spanish were the worst. In 1535, Francesco Sforza died without an heir, leaving the Duchy of Milan without a native ruler. Charles V took it over without fanfare. That move sparked a brief encounter between the Spaniards and the French from 1536 to 1538. A much more significant war involving the Ottoman Empire took place between 1542 and 1546 and then again from 1551 to 1559. Benzoni departed for the Americas in 1551, war breaking out around him again as France and Spain fought for control of his homeland. His anger toward the Spanish and the machinations of Charles V stemmed in part from this experience. Given the scope of conflicts involving the Habsburgs, other Europeans came to adopt similarly negative views of the Spanish.

Although derogatory descriptions of the Spanish have persisted since the sixteenth century, this pattern of national stereotyping received no serious scholarly attention until the twentieth century. In 1914, the Spanish scholar Julián Juderías dubbed the anti-Spanish stereotype the "Black Legend." Since then, scholars have heatedly

18. See Mallett and Shaw, *Italian Wars, 1494–1559*.
19. Lane, *Pillaging the Empire*, chap. 1.

debated the origins and implications of the term.[20] At its core, the Black Legend portrays Spaniards as harsh conquerors and colonizers, ruthless in their dealings with Native Americans and exploitive of the land and people under their rule. The Black Legend and the various stereotypes it comprises must be understood as a historical process. It did not spring into existence suddenly but was shaped by interactions between competing groups in Europe and the Americas. The conflicts that routinely pitted Spain against France, England, or Italian city-states fostered antagonism toward the Spanish, and Spain's colonization of the New World and provided new fuel for older animosities. Benzoni's own bias against Spaniards was probably rooted in the expansion of the Kingdom of Aragon into the Mediterranean and Italian Peninsula in the fifteenth century, a process that encouraged negative stereotypes of the Aragonese as mercenaries and bad Christians.[21] Such views persisted in the sixteenth century in response to Spanish participation in the Italian Wars.[22] These earlier biases, and Benzoni's personal experience in the Italian Wars, preconditioned his view of Spanish conquest in the Americas.

The single most cited source of anti-Spanish stereotypes has been the work of the Spanish conquistador-turned-missionary Bartolomé de Las Casas. Since its initial publication in Spanish in 1552, European rivals have used Las Casas's *Short Account of the Destruction of the Indies* to denounce the cruelty of the Spanish. Benzoni's *History of the New World,* by contrast, is largely unknown to modern audiences. It is tempting to assume that Benzoni's obscurity reflects the later publication of his narrative, which appeared in print thirteen years after Las Casas's *Short Account* captured the attention of European critics. But this is not the case. In fact, Benzoni's *History of the New World* may have reached more European readers in the sixteenth century than the *Short Account* did.

After its initial publication in Italian in 1565, *The History of the New World* was reissued in 1572 and quickly translated and disseminated in Latin (1578), French (1579), German (1579), and Dutch

20. Most notably, between 1969 and 1971, a series of studies contested the historical significance of the legend. See Gibson, *Black Legend;* Keen, "Black Legend Revisited"; Hanke, "Moratorium on Grand Generalizations"; Powell, *Tree of Hate;* Maltby, *Black Legend in England.*
21. Enders and Fraser, "Italian in the New World," 22.
22. Powell, *Tree of Hate,* 41–42.

(1610), as noted above. Las Casas's *Short Account* was not translated until 1578, when it appeared in Dutch. By roughly the same date, Benzoni's *History* was available to Italian, French, and German readers, and educated readers could read it in Latin. By the end of the century, the *Short Account* had gained ground, with translations into French (1579), English (1583), and German (1599). Although the relative size of readership cannot be determined, the popularity of *The History of the New World* certainly rivaled or exceeded that of the *Short Account* during the second half of the sixteenth century.[23]

Nevertheless, in the long sweep of history, Las Casas's writing continued to be mobilized as anti-Spanish propaganda long after Benzoni's *History of the New World* fell into obscurity.[24] One reason for Las Casas's ascendency over the long haul involves the successive republication of the *Short Account* during periods of conflict between Spain and its European rivals. English translations, for example, appeared in 1583, 1625, 1656, 1689, 1699, and 1745. Each of these reprintings coincided with heightened tensions between Spain and England.[25] Between 1552 and 1750, the *Short Account* appeared in at least thirty-four editions, the majority of them published by Spanish rivals. At least fourteen Dutch editions appeared in the seventeenth century alone. By the end of the eighteenth century, six editions had appeared in English and six in French.[26] The staying power of Las Casas's *Short Account* lies in its focused, well-argued, polemical attack on the Spanish conquest and its participants. In contrast, *The History of the New World* mixes critique with travelogue, history, geography, and adventure. While Las Casas relentlessly describes atrocity after atrocity, Benzoni's narrative meanders, jumping between past and present and mixing history, hearsay, and personal anecdotes. While Benzoni's style of writing clearly captured the imagination of sixteenth-century Europeans who sought news from the Americas, by the seventeenth century, Las Casas's brutal direct attack proved more enticing to European readers eager to vilify the Spanish in the midst of international conflict. Benzoni's work faded into obscurity because its style no longer appealed to European

---

23. Keen, "Black Legend Revisited," 712–15.
24. Gibson, *Black Legend*, 14, 17.
25. Keen, "Black Legend Revisited," 717.
26. Powell, *Tree of Hate*, 99.

audiences. Nevertheless, the early fascination with Benzoni makes his *History* a formative source for the development of the Black Legend.

Spanish America Before Benzoni

Although Benzoni's narrative was one of the earliest histories of the Americas, he arrived in the New World almost fifty years after Columbus first claimed Hispaniola for the Spanish. During that half century, many of the most populous societies of the Americas were conquered, among them the Aztecs, Incas, Mayans, and Muiscas. But the Spanish conquests of the Americas were by no means finished, as Benzoni learned firsthand during his travels.

The strategies, tactics, and patterns of Spanish conquest in the Americas did not develop in isolation. For nearly eight hundred years (711–1492), Christian kingdoms in Iberia waged on-again off-again war against Muslim caliphates. These wars were commonly known as the Reconquista (Reconquest) because Christians viewed their struggle as an attempt to conquer areas lost to Muslim conquests of the eighth century. The Reconquista ended in 1492, when Ferdinand and Isabel, co-monarchs of the kingdoms of Castile and Aragon, conquered the last caliphate. The simultaneous ending of the Reconquista and the discovery of the New World allowed for a seamless transition between the conquest of Iberia and conquest in the Americas.

Significantly, the men who fought to expand Spain's territory in the Americas did so as private individuals, not as uniformed soldiers of the king's army.[27] Rather than command a large standing army, Iberian monarchs commissioned individuals, often nobles or wealthy subjects, to raise "companies" of troops. Those who commanded companies of soldiers were promised rewards for successful campaigns that might include noble titles, tax exemptions, political office, or financial remuneration. For example, before setting out on his voyage, Columbus entered into a contractual agreement with Ferdinand and Isabel that stipulated the rewards he would receive for a successful venture. Similar agreements were made between successive prospective conquistadors and the monarchs. The kings of Spain

---

27. Lockhart and Otte, *Letters and People of the Spanish Indies*, 3.

did not finance these expeditions; they promised future rewards for privately organized and funded campaigns.

Conquistadors organized themselves in companies that resembled modern business ventures more than military units. Individuals who joined a company were required to provide some material support to the campaign, and rewards for successful conquests were divided according to the initial investment of the members. The necessity of private financing also ensured that these companies were frequently composed of men of means. Few poor men became conquistadors; most who participated in the conquest had some training as tradesmen or artisans.[28]

Once in the Americas, the Caribbean served as a proving ground where conquistador companies developed methods that would help them better succeed in their intended conquests.[29] These included the search for native allies, the acquisition of translators, the use of terrorism and display violence, and the search for precious metals. The Spanish quickly recognized that indigenous people would always outnumber them, and many expeditions learned to identify local conflicts that could be used to pit one indigenous group against another.[30] In some instances, the cross-cultural dialogue used in these negotiations led Native Americans to ally themselves willingly with the Spanish.[31] We can see many of these tactics in Benzoni's narrative, and they would remain staples of Spanish conquest and colonial rule for centuries.

The Spanish conquest of the Americas proceeded slowly. Between 1492 and 1500, Columbus undertook four voyages and explored the Greater and Lesser Antilles. Few colonists made the transatlantic journey in the fifteenth century, however. Before 1500, most settlement occurred on the island of Hispaniola. The European presence in the Caribbean accelerated after 1502, when the newly appointed royal governor, Nicolás de Ovando, arrived with several thousand

28. Schwaller, with Nader, *First Letter from New Spain*, 244–45.
29. Restall, *Seven Myths of the Spanish Conquest*, 19–26.
30. Examples of this process can be seen in accounts from various campaigns. For examples from the conquest of Mexico, see Schwartz, *Victors and Vanquished*. Two volumes in Penn State Press's LAO series preserve examples from the conquests of Guatemala and Colombia. See Francis, *Invading Colombia;* Restall and Asselbergs, *Invading Guatemala.*
31. See Matthew and Oudijk, *Indian Conquistadors.*

settlers.[32] By 1510, conquest companies had begun to expand into the greater Caribbean. From Hispaniola, expansion took two paths. The first expanded west to Cuba, Jamaica, and eventually the mainland of Mexico and Central America. The second, the path Benzoni followed, expanded east and south to the Lesser Antilles, the northern coastline of South America, Panama, the Pacific, and eventually Peru. Spanish expansion did not merely seek new territory. Rather, conquistadors sought areas with large numbers of Native Americans. Consequently, these two paths of expansion skipped over many areas. Most of the small islands of the Caribbean (e.g., Dominica, Saint Kitts, Grenada) were explored but not conquered during this period because they were sparsely populated and lacked precious resources. Major conquests during this period included Puerto Rico (1508), Jamaica (1509), Panama (1510), and Cuba (1511). Between 1519 and 1521, Hernán Cortés used the typical practices of finding translators, recruiting native allies, and using display violence to forge Spanish-native alliances that would ultimately topple the Aztec Empire. A decade later, between 1532 and 1537, Francisco Pizarro used similar practices to conquer much of the Inca Empire.

Spanish America During Benzoni's Travels (1541–1556)

The publication in Europe of accounts detailing the conquests had increased the pace of immigration to the Americas even as new conquests continued to expand Spanish territorial control. From Mexico, campaigns pushed into northern Mexico (1530s–50s), Guatemala (1520s) and Central America, and eventually Florida (1565). From Peru, conquests expanded south into Chile (1541) and north into Ecuador (1535) and Colombia (1537). During this time, previously overlooked areas received attention, as new arrivals looked to profit from the spoils of conquest. Parts of northern South America were settled as explorers discovered pearl fisheries and gold deposits. Atlantic exploration led to the settlement of Buenos Aires (1536). From there, conquests traveled inland into Paraguay (1537) and Bolivia (1548).

During Benzoni's travels, major political changes would gradually slow the pace of conquest and seek to rein in the power of the

---

32. See Sauer, *Early Spanish Main*, chap. 7.

conquistadors and early settlers. In most areas, the lead conquistador, or *adelantado*, became the first governor of conquered regions. As governors, *adelantados* were allowed to appoint other officials, grant lands, and collect taxes. Additionally, these conquistador-governors rewarded many of their soldiers with *encomienda* grants. Based on an older model from the Reconquest, *encomiendas* granted individual conquistadors the right to demand tribute and labor from specific indigenous communities. Over time, the Spanish monarchs worked to replace conquistador-governors with officials of their choosing. In some cases, accusations of malfeasance or the mistreatment of indigenous subjects served as a pretext for the appointment of new royal officials.[33] In most cases, the transitions went smoothly, but on occasion, the attempt to assert royal authority could lead to civil war. In 1544, following the appointment of new officials and the promulgation of new legislation limiting the power of conquistadors over Native Americans, the conquistadors of Peru rose up in rebellion, killing the newly arrived viceroy.[34]

Although Benzoni arrived after the major conquests of Mexico and Peru, he was present during a crucial period in Spanish American history. Established regions were transitioning from frontier settlements to major urban centers. New conquests expanded the frontier into previously uncharted territory. Politically, the region became more centralized, as royal authority sought to establish new, uniform systems of government. Benzoni's writing provides a unique vista into the diversity of experience during this turbulent period.

Native Americans Before and After Conquest

Like many other early chroniclers of the Americas, Benzoni recorded a great deal of information about Native Americans. Although most Europeans called indigenous residents of the Americas *indios*, in the mistaken belief that Columbus had discovered India/Asia, among *indios* there existed a huge diversity of culture. In some areas, like

33. This process began with Columbus himself, who was removed from office as governor in 1500 and replaced with a royal appointee, Francisco de Bobadilla. Ibid., 102–7.

34. Lockhart, *Spanish Peru*, 3–5.

Mesoamerica and the Andes, Native Americans practiced agriculture and lived in large urban settlements.[35] In other regions, especially the Caribbean islands and northern South America, Native Americans eschewed large urban areas. Although they were often agriculturalists, the settlement pattern in these regions was more dispersed, and communities could range from several dozen households to several thousand people.[36] The social and cultural diversity of Native Americans played an important role in their interaction with Spaniards and Spanish colonialism. In all areas, Spaniards sought to negotiate with local leaders and identify local rivalries. Through these contacts, Spaniards gained vital information about the human landscape. In some instances, this process led native groups to accept Spanish authority without open conflict. In other cases, initial contact led to hostilities.

Conquistadors viewed *indios* as sources of labor and tribute. Through the use of the *encomienda*, individual Spaniards were allowed to demand labor—often for the mining of precious metals—and tribute from native subjects. In imposing the burdens of tribute and forced labor, the Spanish frequently exempted indigenous elites, especially *caciques* (local rulers).[37] This practice helped to forge ties between the indigenous elites and the Spanish, ties that were sometimes furthered through marriage when conquistadors married the daughters of *caciques*.[38]

The patterns of conquest and exploitation that began in the Caribbean expanded to the mainland. Among the more populous and urban societies of Mesoamerica and the Andes, however, the imposition of Spanish authority frequently benefited from existing social and political structures.[39] Consequently, Spanish colonialism appropriated rather than replaced existing forms of imperial control in those areas. As in the Caribbean, preferential status was given to local elites to help facilitate the transition from pre-Columbian empires to Spanish imperialism.

35. For research on pre-Columbian urban life, see Sanders, Guadalupe Mastache, and Cobean, *Urbanismo en Mesoamérica;* Moore, *Architecture and Power.*

36. See Sued-Badillo, "Indigenous Societies."

37. The Spanish appropriated the term *cacique* from the Arawak language of the Caribbean. Through Spanish colonialism, its use spread throughout the Americas.

38. For a concise discussion of these marriages and their offspring, see Kuznesof, "Ethnic and Gender Influences."

39. For example, see Lockhart, *Nahuas After the Conquest.*

Almost immediately, the Spaniards who held *encomienda* grants were criticized for their abuse of indigenous subjects, the most vocal opposition coming from Spanish clergymen. In 1511, Antonio de Montesino, a Dominican friar, preached an impassioned sermon that criticized the residents of Santo Domingo for their mistreatment of indigenous subjects. "Tell me," he challenged them, "what right have you to enslave them? What authority did you use to make war against them who lived at peace on their territories, killing them cruelly with methods never before heard of? Aren't they human beings? Have they no rational soul? . . . You may rest assured that you are in no better state of salvation than the Moors or the Turks who reject the Christian faith."[40] The sermon sparked outrage among the early settlers; some complained to the king and queen. Incensed by the settlers' actions, the monarchs sided with Montesino and issued the first laws regulating the exploitation of Native Americans, the Laws of Burgos (1512). Although these laws sought to restrict the rampant exploitation of Native Americans, such abuse continued, especially in newly conquered areas and fringe zones. By the 1540s, the continued abuse of native subjects, combined with the desire to limit the power of settlers, led the monarchy to issue a more expansive set of laws to protect Native Americans. The New Laws (1542) banned the enslavement and conscription to mines of *indios* and outlawed the inheritance of *encomienda* grants, among other provisions.

Over the course of the sixteenth century, royal legislation gradually created a unique legal and political sphere for indigenous subjects.[41] Although *indios* were always required to pay tribute and were prohibited from holding many political and ecclesiastical offices, they were also considered special subjects of the king and were granted many rights denied to other non-Spanish groups, such as Africans and people of mixed race. Native communities were allowed self-governance, exemption from the Inquisition, and special royal officials to protect their interests and investigate abuses. Benzoni's writings provide glimpses into the complex relationship between Spaniards and Native Americans and help illustrate the disjuncture between legal norms and everyday practices.

40. Quoted in Las Casas, *History of the Indies*, 184.
41. See Góngora, *Estado en el derecho indiano*; Zavala, *Instituciones jurídicas*; Kellogg, *Transformation of Aztec Culture*; Owensby, *Empire of Law*.

Just as Spanish law reacted to the abuses of indigenous subjects, intellectuals continued to debate the issues raised by Antonio de Montesino in 1511. In 1551, Bartolomé de Las Casas met with Juan de Sepúlveda, a humanist scholar who specialized in ancient Greek philosophy, in the Spanish city of Valladolid to discuss the viability of Indian self-rule.[42] Sepúlveda used Aristotle and the Bible to argue that the Indians were natural slaves; Las Casas responded, using the same sources, that the indigenous were free men entitled to humane treatment. Though the debate was theoretical and brought no immediate concrete changes in policy, it demonstrated contemporary concerns in Europe about the treatment of indigenous people. Some scholars argue that the debate at Valladolid set the stage for later anticolonial thought.[43]

The first edition of Benzoni's *Historia* came out not long after the Valladolid debate and contributed to a growing European awareness of the atrocities committed under colonial expansion. Moreover, the interest in the emancipation and rights of non-Europeans did not end with the abuse of Native Americans. Abolition movements would become quite popular in Europe in the seventeenth and eighteenth centuries, mobilizing similar arguments about Africans' humanity.[44] The sensational atrocities of the Spanish certainly contributed to the monumental sales of Benzoni and Las Casas, and their firsthand accounts of the mistreatment of Indians probably fed antislavery sentiments.

Although Benzoni frequently sides with Native Americans against what he perceives (or at least portrays) as the savage Spanish, cannibalism is a recurring theme in his *History*. The attribution of cannibalism to some Native American groups began almost as soon as the Spanish arrived in the Caribbean. This accusation served the interest of Spanish conquistadors, because, unlike the so-called civilized groups, cannibals could be dealt with more harshly. When legislation began to limit the enslavement of native peoples, exceptions were made for cannibals. In the early colonization of the Caribbean, these distinctions were mapped onto the ethnic markers applied to indigenous groups. *Caribs* were labeled cannibals and subjected

42. See Hanke, *All Mankind Is One;* Las Casas, *In Defense of the Indians.*
43. See, for example, Keen, "Legacy of Bartolomé de Las Casas."
44. For a good treatment of abolition movements, see Peabody, *There Are No Slaves in France.*

to enslavement, while *Aruacas* (Arawaks) were not cannibals and therefore enjoyed legal protections. Significantly, this early distinction between "good" and "bad" *indios*, a view clearly perpetuated by Benzoni's *History*, had lasting consequences in obscuring the cultural landscape of the early Americas.[45]

In the pages that follow, the reader is carried along on a journey of discovery, adventure, and at times political intrigue. Benzoni's rich descriptions capture the Spanish colonial world during a unique moment, poised between initial conquests and colonial maturity. We are given glimpses of unexplored frontiers and bustling port cities, wild jungles and burgeoning plantations, unconquered Indians and rebellious African slaves. Ultimately, *The History of the New World* was a massive success, offering European readers new and varied stories about the New World while grounding itself in the politics and culture of the Old.

Notes on the Translation

Every translation necessarily involves some interpretation, and this one is no exception. We have omitted various segments of Benzoni's narrative, in part to keep the text a manageable length. Mostly, we cut long and repetitive accounts rehashing earlier conquistadors' exploits that add little to Benzoni's tale; we note these expunctions in the footnotes. The abridgement remains faithful to Benzoni's overall narrative and its focus on his travels and firsthand experiences. We chose to translate the second edition, published by Piero and Franceso Tini in 1572. There are few substantive differences between the 1565 and 1572 editions, but the latter had a much larger run. It is thus not only the edition that most early moderns would have read but the one most accessible to modern scholars.

Benzoni wrote in vernacular Italian and generally used Italian names in his text. We have rendered these names in their appropriate languages: usually Spanish, some French, and occasionally a version of the local indigenous language. When Benzoni takes his turn as a lexicographer and lists the local words, we have generally left them as he wrote them; these words appear italicized in the text. Benzoni used

45. See Whitehead, *Lords of the Tiger Spirit* and *Of Cannibals and Kings*.

signori, an Italian title of respect for men equivalent to the English *gentlemen,* to refer to indigenous rulers. This parallels the Spanish use of *señores* for such individuals. In the text, *signori* has been translated as *lords* to match the Spanish convention. Benzoni also used the idiomatic *Mori* (Moors), in reference to all Africans and people of African descent in the New World, regardless of their actual place of origin. His use of the term is equivalent to the modern use of *black.* Finally, Benzoni uses some measurements that are no longer in standard use. We have left these in the text and explained them in the notes.

Benzoni was not a gifted writer. As the reader will see, the finer points of metaphor, well-placed adjectives, and a clever turn of phrase never interrupt his narrative. Instead, Benzoni reports and assesses experiences in straightforward prose. Sadly, this devotion to the story at the expense of literary niceties makes his work less clear than one might hope. At times, clarity is obscured by Benzoni's firm belief that a series of subordinate clauses constitutes a sentence, and by his reliance on completely idiosyncratic vocabulary. In places, we have radically altered his sentence structure, replaced pronouns with proper nouns and vice versa, and added verbs for the purpose of clarity. The aim has been to preserve his meaning and tone while rendering the text more readable.

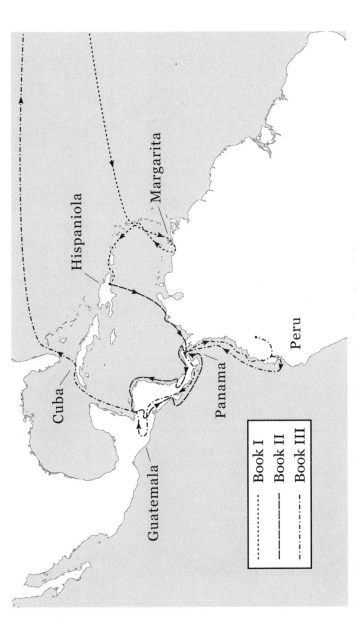

Benzoni's travels, 1541–1556. The route of Benzoni's travels as described in the *Historia del Mondo Nuovo*. Map by Robert C. Schwaller.

THE HISTORY OF THE
NEW WORLD

Book I

Being young, only twenty-two, and desiring to see the world like many others, and having heard word of the new countries just discovered in the Indies many call the New World, I determined to go. And so I left Milan in 1541. I went overland to Medina del Campo where the great markets and fairs of all Spain are held. And after that I went to Seville, and then went down the river Guadalquivir, where I was taken to Sanlúcar de Barrameda, which is the main port for the whole navy, with all the ships that come and go from the Indies.[1] I found a ship that was leaving, full of goods for the island of Gran Canaria. I got on because I had not found a shorter route for my trip. I had heard that in these seven islands you could always find ships loaded with wine, flour, apples, cheese, and other necessities for the territories. So I booked the trip and after two months I arrived. Once I got there, I heard that a caravel in Palma was being loaded with wine to go to the Indies. So I headed there immediately in a ship, arrived in two days, and we set sail.

After traveling with good winds for fourteen days, we saw a large flock of seabirds, so we realized with great happiness that we must be near land. Many times during the night some fish of about a palm[2] in size, with wings like birds, flew into the boat. The pilot had begun to take the sun's attitude at noon and at night by the North Star, which was already very low. After two days sailing like this, on a Sunday

1. Sanlúcar de Barrameda served as a primary port of departure for the Americas. Benzoni uses the term *navy* to describe the large number of civilian merchant ships operating between Spain and its American colonies.

2. The palm is an old Mediterranean measurement equal to the approximate length of an adult male's hand, roughly eight to ten inches.

morning around sunrise, we saw land. The captain of the ship told me that this was the very island that the invincible Christopher Columbus arrived at before taking off for the Spanish islands in his caravel after 24 or 25 days on his second voyage from the Canaries without having seen land. He wanted to see it so much that he named the island Desiderata.[3]

There were many islands, but the largest the Spanish had was called Guadalupe. The largest part of this island was full of Carib Indians who eat one another. That is to say, they eat their enemies. We saw a ship of Indian fishermen who fled when they saw us. We continued on our trip, heading slightly left, toward the equinoctial line. We saw some other islands at the end of eight days. There we found Cubagua and the governor Jerónimo de Ortal. He had me stay with him, offering me great profit, as governors do. He told me that he wanted to put together an expedition with a lot of Spaniards to an area named Nautal (now called El Dorado because it is so full of great riches), saying that if we went we would all be very rich. So, because of these grand promises and some others he made, I stayed. I was curious about the country and I wanted to be very rich.

Not long after, others arrived in Cubagua. Pedro de Herrera, the governor of the island of Margarita, came with two brigs, accompanied by thirty Spaniards who intended to go through the territory to pick up some slaves.[4] So, shortly after, one morning about two hours after sunrise, we left together with Jerónimo de Ortal. In the evening we arrived at the river of Cumaná, where there was a wooden fort built by the Spanish to protect the boats that came from Cubagua for water. There used to be an earthen fort with pearl fisheries, but one time the river rose because of the rains and overflowed in such a way that more than two miles of countryside in every direction was flooded and the fort was destroyed. There were still a few little houses, four or five, made of reeds where the captain, Diego de Ocampo, had built the city of Toledo (as we called it).[5]

3.   There are dozens of islands in the Lesser Antilles whose names have changed repeatedly in the intervening years; this is one of them. If it was the first island Columbus sighted on his second voyage, it is probably Dominica.

4.   After 1542, the process of raiding for Native American slaves was outlawed in New Spain. Andrien, *Andean Worlds*, 44. Herrera's actions are not surprising, as the New Laws were frequently ignored.

5.   Gonzalo de Ocampo founded Nuevo Toledo in 1520. Humbert, *Historia de Colombia y de Venezuela*, 71.

Indiana marauigliofa in Cumana.

FIG. 1 Wondrous woman in Cumaná. "Indiana marauigliosa in Cumana."
In Benzoni, *La historia del Mondo Nuovo*, 1565. Courtesy of the John Carter
Brown Library at Brown University.

While we were in Cumaná, an Indian woman, a wife of a chief of
one of the major provinces, arrived with a sack full of fruit. She was
like nothing I had ever seen before and I could not stop staring at her
in wonder. She entered the governor's tent, sat down on a bench, and
put her fruit down in front of him without saying a word. And she
looked like this:

She was completely naked except for her shameful parts, as was
the custom. She was old and painted black, with long hair down to
her waist and earrings so huge that her ears hung down to her shoulders. Her ears were a wonder. She had split them down the middle
and filled them with light carved wood, which they call *cacoma*. Her
nails were extremely long, her teeth were black, and her mouth was

very large. She had a ring in her nose, which they call a *caricori*. To us she looked more monster than human.[6]

After two days we left Cumaná, and headed east to the Gulf of Paria.[7] We stopped often to gift friendly chiefs with wine, or clothes, or a knife from the governor, and convinced them to send some of their men to show us places in the countryside where we could capture their enemies. The governor stayed at Cariaco with eight Spaniards. The rest of us followed our friendly native allies, who carried our provisions inland about one hundred miles, through valleys, mountains, rivers, woods, and other places where the guides led. We went through holes and over cliffs where even wolves would have been scared. We traveled more often at night and we captured over 240 slaves, men and women, small and large.[8]

The captain was worried we would run out of food, even though we had taken some from the Indians, so we turned back. One morning near Alba we saw two fires, one in the mountains and the other in a valley. We split the company in two and went in different directions. The group that had gone down to the valley arrived first and found only one old woman, her daughter, and her granddaughter sleeping quietly. When the Spaniards tried to grab them, they woke them all, and the women screamed so loudly that the natives on the hill heard and started to yell in response. This so scared our people that they ran back to join us.

Our enemies ran ahead to the passes we were heading for. Daylight was coming and they saw that there were many more of us than they thought (and that we were armed), so they retreated. That did not keep them from harassing us with darts, and calling us thieves, dogs, traitors, and assassins. I believe that if not for our native friends, who made them run off, we would have sustained great injury and ruin. We left without loss. We left the old woman because she could not walk, and in two days we rejoined the governor. We rested a few

6. This depiction of indigenous women as monstrous perpetuates a long European pattern of using female bodies as a means of highlighting the savagery and barbarism of non-Europeans. Morgan, "'Some Could Suckle,'" 170–74.

7. Located between Venezuela and the island of Trinidad.

8. Despite the 1542 prohibition of indigenous slave raiding, the Spanish organizers of these raids appear to have considered them "just wars" fought against belligerent natives who waged war on indigenous allies of the Spanish.

days, then proceeded along the coast about eighty miles in boats used in that country, called *pirague*.[9] The largest seat about fifty people.

All along the coast the Indians come down from the hills to fish. We would hide ourselves under cover and wait all day to capture them. When they arrived we would jump on them like wolves attacking sheep and make them slaves. We captured about fifty, mostly women and small children. Eventually we went to a place where we were discovered by some of our enemies, who were fishing. They yelled loudly and alerted all of the others to our presence. They all ran away and all we could get was some fish that had been dried on a reed fire and some sun-dried grasshoppers, which these people string up in rows for easier transportation home.

The captain then saw that we couldn't capture any more men and turned back. He took us to the house of a poor little chieftain who was friendly to the Spanish, and gave him a bottle of wine, a shirt, and a few knives, and with good words asked if he would like to take us to a place where we could capture some slaves. The chieftain didn't want to take Christians with him, but took a party of his own men and returned a few days later with sixteen Indians, with their hands tied behind their backs. He gave them to our captain, who thanked him profusely, and promised to return again with bigger and better gifts.

And so we returned to Cariaco. The next day we reached Cumaná. The governor sent the slaves off to Cubagua and sent his native friends home. On the way, the Indians were attacked by their enemies and four were killed. The rest came back to Cumaná to beg the governor for an armed escort of Christians to return with them and take revenge on their common enemy. The governor showed great sorrow for their loss but said that he could not help as he and his men had bigger business to attend to in other places. He promised that he would help another time. The Indians left in a state of great discontent, with angry words for the Christians and their thieving, which was the cause of their ruin.

The governor quickly left Cumaná with all of his company, heading westward to Amaracapanna, which was a city of about 40 houses.[10]

9. *Piragua* (Spanish), a type of dugout canoe common to the Circum-Caribbean.
10. Near Píritu, Venezuela.

About 400 Spaniards lived there year round and they elected a captain annually. The governor and about half his solders went scavenging through several provinces of the country, taking many friends who lived near the gulf with them. While we were in Amaracapanna, Captain Pedro de Cáliz arrived with more than 4,000 slaves. He had captured many more but they had died on the journey from hunger, overwork, and exhaustion, as well as from sorrow at leaving their country, their fathers, their mothers, or their children. When some of the slaves could not walk, the Spaniards tried to prevent them from making war later by burying their swords in their sides or in their breasts.

It was really an upsetting thing to see the way these sad, naked, tired, and lame creatures were treated. They were exhausted with hunger, illness, and sadness. The unlucky mothers were all tied with rope or chains around their necks or arms and had two or three children, overcome with tears of grief, hanging around their necks or on their shoulders. Nor was there a woman who had not been violated by the predators. Because there were so many Spaniards who indulged their lust, many were left broken. This captain had gone 700 miles inland into a country that was full of people when the Spanish arrived, but by the time I arrived very little was left undestroyed.

The Spaniards fight on horseback with the Indians in these provinces. They wear a doublet, generously lined with cotton wool, and carry a lance and a sword.[11] Those on foot carry a small round shield, a sword, and a crossbow, and wear a light doublet. They do not carry an arquebus, chain armor, or a breastplate because of the humidity.[12] They often have to sleep out in the open and the wetness would ruin them quickly.

I believe that most of the countryside south of Paria is the most beautiful and fruitful of any I have seen in any part of the Indies. It has a large and fertile plain where there are always flowers, some that smell nice and some with a terrible odor. The trees are perpetually in bloom as if it were always spring, though not all of them bear fruit. In some parts there is medicinal *cassia*. The province is usually hot and damp and full of mosquitoes that are very annoying at night. There are also swarms of locusts that harm the plants severely.

11.   Most Spaniards wore light leather jerkins or padded cotton doublets for their ease of movement and lighter weight. Hassig, *Mexico and the Spanish Conquest*, 88.
12.   The harquebus was an early muzzle-loaded firearm.

The men wear a codpiece shaped like a cannon made of squash that covers their manhood and leaves the rest to hang freely. The codpieces used to be covered in pearls and gold but the Spanish put a stop to that. Married women cover their shameful parts with a cloth called a *pamanilia*. The young girls wear only a cord. Wealthy lords are allowed to take as many wives as they want, but only one is legitimate.[13] She commands all the others. The poorer people only take three or four and they get rid of them when they get older so they can take younger wives. Each of the wives are deflowered by holy men called *piacchi*.[14]

Their main food source is fish. They also make wine out of maize and out of other various fruits and roots. They eat human flesh, and spiders, worms, other disgusting things, and lice, like the monkeys. They make a rare mixture out of oyster shells—the kind that make pearls—that they char with the leaves of the *axi* tree to preserve their teeth. They temper these with a little water and spread it over their teeth, which become as black as charcoal, but then are conserved forever without pain. They pierce their nostrils, lips, and ears. They paint their body with the juice of red and black herbs. Really, the uglier they become, the more beautiful they think they are.

The beds of the principal lords are made with a tarp, longer than it is wide, like a sheet. The tarp is suspended in the air on two large poles, and they sleep on that.[15] Those who sleep in the countryside keep a large fire burning continuously so they won't get cold. This is the normal way of sleeping in all the provinces.

The principal arms they carry are bows with two kinds of poisoned arrows, either of palm wood or of a kind of reeds that grow by the river.[16] Instead of iron tips they use hard fish scales and pieces of flint covered with a black cement which is pure venom made from roots, herbs, ants, apples, and some other beastly mixture combined and boiled with difficulty and diligence by the old women. The vapor

13. Polygamy among indigenous leaders played a key role in political alliances. Benzoni's statement exaggerates the frequency of the practice, particularly among commoners. Sued-Badillo, "Indigenous Societies," 268.

14. *Piaii* or *piache*, a religious leader or shaman. *Piaches* were allowed to take multiple wives. Whitehead, *Lords of the Tiger Spirit*, 62–63.

15. A hammock, from the Taíno *hamaka*.

16. For a more detailed description of Carib warfare, see Whitehead, "Snake Warriors."

Modo di dormire nel Golfo di Paria, & altri molti luoghi.

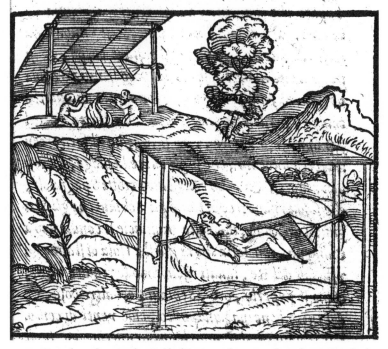

FIG. 2 How they sleep in the Gulf of Paria, and many other places. "Modo di dormire nel Golfo di Paria, & altri molti luoghi." In Benzoni, *La historia del Mondo Nuovo*, 1565. Courtesy of the John Carter Brown Library at Brown University.

that comes from it is so dangerous that most of the women die. When the tincture is fresh, the man who was wounded by this arrow swells and is so hurt that he goes mad and dies quickly. If the poison is old it loses its efficacy, so the wounded can be remedied by lancing the swollen place with a red-hot iron. I have known several Spaniards who were saved this way.

All the slaves that the Spaniards take in this province are hauled to Cubagua, home of the king's offices that collect royal taxes of twenty percent on pearls, gold, slaves, and other things. They brand the slaves on the face and arms with a letter C and then the governors and captains do what they please with them.[17] Sometimes they give them to the soldiers, who periodically sell them or gamble them away to one another. When the Spanish ships arrive, they trade the slaves for wine, flour, biscuits, and other necessities. The merchants then send the slaves to the island of Hispaniola or take them elsewhere and sell them. They fill the caravels with them, keeping them below decks. Because almost all of them were captured inland, the sea tortures them. Not being able to move there, under the cargo hold, they stand in vomit and the results of their other needs like animals. And when the sea is calm they lack water and other necessities. They are made miserable by the heat and the stink and the thirst and the close quarters until they die wretchedly.

Today all of the country around the Gulf of Paria and other places are empty of the Spaniards. Because there are no more pearls, gold, or fish, they have no other income except slaves. There are few of them since the governor has given the Indians their freedom, so most Spaniards have gone to other countries.

An order from the royal court at Santo Domingo arrived a few days after we returned to Amaracapanna. It demanded that Governor Jerónimo de Ortal be seized and taken safely to Hispaniola for some crime that he committed. And so he abandoned his promise to take me on a voyage and make me rich.

Also, after changing landscape and food, and because of the great heat and poor sleep, and because I had absorbed so much moisture from the ground, I got sick.[18] And if not for a noble French priest named Antoine de Castile, who was loved, honored, and even revered by everyone for his honesty and his openness (and also because he was such a handsome specimen), I would have died. Truly, I would have done really poorly except he made me get on a boat at Amaracapanna and sent me to wait for him at Isla Margarita, where he had his farm and most of his slaves. He treated me with such care as if I were his own son. He took care of me for about six months until

---

17. The "C" brand may have represented a stylized crown, typically done when royal taxes on the slave had been paid.

18. Benzoni based his self-diagnosis on humoral theory, which posited that health and temperament were based on the balance of the four humors of the body (blood, phlegm, yellow bile, and black bile).

I was healthy. And when I was ready to leave we parted as good friends. He gave me everything I needed for my trip.

So I boarded a caravel full of slaves. We sailed along the coast of Cabo de la Vela, and then crossed the sea—with much trouble because of the calm—until we arrived at the island of Boricua, which the Spanish call San Juan of Puerto Rico because of the abundance of gold and silver they found there. When the Spaniards first conquered this island, the Indians believed they were immortal. One of the principal lords of the island decided to try this out and sent some of his servants to capture a Spaniard and bring him back. They carried him to the river and held him under the water for long enough that if he were mortal he would drown. And so they put the drowned man on their shoulders and carried him to their lord. Seeing that he was dead, the lord surmised that the others were also mortal. He got together with the other leaders and rose up against the Spanish and killed about 150 of them who were spread out over the island looking for gold.[19] If the Spanish had not been joined by Diego de Salazar, with reinforcements, they all would have been cut into pieces.[20] We rested for a bit, then departed for Hispaniola, quickly reached it, and entered the town of Santo Domingo. This was the first town the Spaniards built in this country.

Before I go on, I want to tell you all about the opinions these Indians held of the Christians when they appeared in the New World.[21] When the Spaniards first arrived in the Indies, in many places—especially in the mainland provinces of the north—the Indians were astonished and had great admiration for them. They talked among themselves, wondering where these strange, bearded creatures came from. They saw the swords and the way they dressed, the ships, sails, thick ropes, anchors, and they stood with their mouths hanging open at such a spectacle. They stared and stared again, talking among themselves; everyone had an opinion. Some said a storm must have driven them to shore. Some who heard the guns thought the people who ruled the thunder in the clouds must have descended from the

19. This uprising occurred in 1511, in the Spanish settlement of Sotomayor, present-day Aguada.

20. Diego de Salazar was a lieutenant of Juan Ponce de León, the conquistador of Puerto Rico.

21. Portions of the text have been omitted here, namely, tales of the foundation of Santo Domingo and some stories about Columbus in both the New World and upon his return to Spain.

heavens to see the earth. Others kept their mouths closed, confused and unsure what to say about such a strange new people. In some places they were welcomed as a novelty, but in other places they were not welcomed at all, the people thinking that they saw in their faces something fierce and judging that their friendship would only come at great cost and be of little to no benefit. When the Spaniards came ashore there, the natives wounded them with darts and stones and even killed them. They made them run back to their boats in a hurry. But where they were pleased to see them, the Indian lords humbled themselves and begged and pleaded with the Spaniards to visit their people. Each of them hoped that they would come to their house and they all took great pleasure in bringing them food and drinks.

The Spaniards had their eyes on some of the Indians who wore pearls at their necks or wrists. They were upset that they had none. They noticed that the Indians were up to their noses in jewelry with gold, turquoise, and emeralds.[22] They began to ask for some. Since the Indians did not believe these things to be precious, they gave a great quantity to everyone, like a crude and naïve people. In this friendly exchange, the Indians and the Spaniards got to know one another. The Indians wanted to know where the Spaniards were from and what type of people they were. The Spaniards responded that they were a type called Christians, sent by the son of God, creator of the heavens and the earth, and designated by the king of Castile, and the pope, vicar of the heavenly savior, to notify the world of important things, and that very soon they would be going back where they came from. The Indians, believing what they were told, held this to be the truth. Thinking that they would never again see them, many Indians came every day to see them and considered themselves blessed if they were able to touch them or give them something.

Then the Indians saw that after these Spaniards left others came, and they were already building houses so they could stay in their country. They treated the Indians badly. It was not enough just to ask about gold and demand pearls and precious stones. They also subjected them to torments and abuse. The Indians started to say that these actions did not correspond to their words: the Spaniards said that they were the sons of God but instead they must have an

22. Spaniards prized emeralds as well as gold and silver. See Lane, *Colour of Paradise*, 50–59.

evil master. God would not allow them to act like this: depriving the Indians of their liberty, forcing them into servitude, and killing them. They used good words but performed bad deeds. There were some among the Indians who said, "What God can this be who has created such terrible sons, such wicked men? If the sons take after the father, then he cannot be good." They said this and things like this.

If the Spaniards, when they first entered this country, had acted with kindness, and then continued to act with kindness and meekness, instead of acting with cruelty and avarice, I have to believe that this generation of brute savages would have learned to live with reason, and would have been given virtue and honor, and earned the name Christians. Then we would not have seen the death of so many Spaniards, or the destruction of such multitudes of Indians, as you will hear later in this history. Instead of bearing us continual hatred and abusing us, they would have loved and revered us.

Eight friars came from Santo Domingo and built a monastery in Cumaná, and another in Amaracapanna, and so went among the Indians to teach the doctrine of our faith.[23] They taught the sons of some of the principal lords to read and to write. Then all the Indians showed general friendship to the Spaniards, and let them go wherever they wanted, so much so that the Spaniards went as far as three hundred miles inland from the coast searching for gold, pearls, and other stuffs without fear.

While all of this was happening in Cumaná, the Doctor Bartolomé de Las Casas, a priest who lived in Santo Domingo, heard of the abundance of pearls harvested in Cubagua, and of the fertility of the countryside, and of the cruelty of the Spaniards toward the natives. So he went to Spain to the court.[24] After the death of King Ferdinand of Spain, Prince Charles was named emperor and crowned Charles the Fifth.[25] And so de Las Casas asked him for the governorship of Cumaná. He informed him of the ills and the terrible treatment that the Indians of the territory received every day as a result of the rapacious greed of the Spanish soldiers. And he said that because of this

23. The narrative picks up here after another lengthy omission in which Benzoni relates stories of Columbus's fourth voyage, his return to Spain, and his subsequent death. He also explains how Christopher's son Diego founded the city of Toledo.

24. Las Casas returned to Spain in 1515.

25. Charles would not become Holy Roman Emperor until 1520. At the time that Las Casas met with Charles, he reigned as King Charles I of Castile and Aragón.

all the Spaniards who were in the provinces were killed. But he said that if he were to go, he could mitigate all the scandalous behavior and would treat the Indians so well that he would be lauded by all of them. Above all, he would augment royal revenue.

But then Doctor Luis Zapata, and others who were involved in the government of the Indies, contradicted this information,[26] judging de Las Casas an inept and vain man, unfit for this enterprise, of little merit, and unaware of the affairs of that nation. Despite all the opposition, de Las Casas got his wish. He had great favor at court from some Flemish men, some other lords, and especially from the emperor's secretary, the count of Nanso.[27] They affirmed that de Las Casas was a good Christian, and would convert the Indians to the service of God and to the benefit of his Majesty, more than anyone else who would go, and that he would send a great quantity of pearls to Spain. Then he asked for three hundred workers to help with the fishing, so as to not overwork the Indians. And so these men would go more willingly, he begged his Majesty to outfit them with a red cross, much like that of Calatrava.[28] The emperor, moved by these good recommendations, gave the doctor all that he wanted.

Most of the Indians on this coast had the custom of eating humans.[29] Some of them opted out of eating the Spaniards because they feared that Spanish bodies might do them harm. When they captured Spaniards alive, especially the captains, they tied their hands and feet, threw them to the ground, and dripped gold in their mouths, saying: "Eat! Eat gold, Christian!" To better humiliate and torture them, some Indians cut an arm, or a shoulder, or a leg off a Spaniard with a flint knife and roasted it on the embers. Then they ate it while dancing and singing. They hung the bones in their temples or in the houses of their lords as trophies of victory.

---

26. Luis Zapata was a *licenciado*, not a doctor, but he did serve on the king's governing councils.

27. The secretary of Charles V was Francisco de los Cobos y Molina, who was not a count.

28. The Order of Calatrava was the oldest military order in Castile. Its emblem was a Greek cross in gules with fleurs-de-lis at its ends.

29. This description follows a considerable omission in which Benzoni narrates secondhand tales about indigenous barbarities, particularly cannibalism. He recounts many horrors that the Spaniards inflicted on the Indians and describes missionaries' attempts to rein in the most egregious of the conquistadors. He also narrates Pizarro's conquest of Peru and the foundation of Darien, Panama.

Come gli Indiani colauano l'oro in bocca a gli Spagnuoli, e dell'habito che lor portano in diuerfi lochi di terra Ferma.

FIG. 3 How the Indians poured gold into the mouths of the Spaniards and the clothes they wear in many places on the mainland. "Come gli Indiani colauano l'oro in bocca a gli Spagnuoli. . . ." In Benzoni, *La historia del Mondo Nuovo*, 1565. Courtesy of the John Carter Brown Library at Brown University.

Many governors and captains came to these islands and to the mainland, all of them looking to become important through the power of great riches. Of those, some were eaten by Indians. Others were killed by other Spaniards because they would not consent to their thievery against the Indians. Others drowned at sea. Others were driven by their thirst for gold so far inland that they ran into deserts. Not knowing the constellations or the patterns of the weather in this country, like how cruel and destructive the winter rains could be, they were unable to go forward or to come back and they died there in the desert with all their followers.

Because I have promised to shorten this text, my short history, in the best way possible, I will return to the story of the island of Hispaniola and the others in that area.[30] When Columbus died, the king, Don Ferdinand, sent Diego, the son of the admiral, to serve as viceroy to Hispaniola with the same authority that he had granted to his father. But that did not last long. The Spaniards could not stand to be commanded by a foreigner in any way, so they wrote many terrible things about him to the king. The king took the governorship from him and called him back to Spain. Diego argued with the king for many years about his privileges and eventually died without having his affairs settled at all.[31] After that, others were sent to Hispaniola, some priests, some not. Eventually the islanders saw that there was intolerable and unbearable labor and oppression from every side, with no chance of ever again regaining their liberty. With sighs and tears they longed for death.

Many of the dispirited Indians went to the woods and hanged themselves after having first killed their children, saying it is better that they die than live miserably, serving men like these horrible thieves and ferocious tyrants. The women used an herbal potion to end their pregnancies and then they joined their husbands and hanged themselves. Some people threw themselves from a mountain down a precipice, and others threw themselves into the sea or a river. Others let themselves die of hunger. Some killed themselves with their flint knives and others shoved sharpened stakes through their chests or sides. Between those who killed themselves, the oppressive work, and the cruelty of the Spanish, so many died that eventually, of the two million Indians who were on the island, not 150 can still be found.[32] This was the way the Christians acted when they arrived on these islands; all the others felt just the same, in Cuba, in Jamaica,

30. Benzoni includes a list of cities founded by the Spaniards.

31. Benzoni's account exaggerates the plight of Diego Colón, probably in order to play up the nationalist critique of the Spanish. Diego Colón had inherited the title "Admiral of the Ocean Sea" upon his father's death, and he served as "Governor of the Indies" from 1509 to 1511. From 1511 to 1523, he held the title "Viceroy of the Indies." Between 1515 and 1520, complaints from Hispaniola led to his being called to court. He retained his titles and returned to govern the island for three more years before finally being removed in 1523. For more on Diego Colón, see Arranz, *Don Diego Colón*.

32. Like other early chroniclers, Benzoni assumes that Spanish abuse caused the catastrophic demographic collapse of indigenous people. Observers could not fathom

Indiani della Spagnuola per non feruire a
i Chriftiani, fi andauano a impiccare alli bofchi.

FIG. 4 The Indians of Hispaniola hang themselves from trees so they do not have to serve the Christians. "Indiani della Spagnuola per non seruire a i Christiani, si andauano a impiccare alli boschi." In Benzoni, *La historia del Mondo Nuovo*, 1565. Courtesy of the John Carter Brown Library at Brown University.

Puerto Rico, and other places. And again it was the same with the slaves brought from the mainland to these islands. There were an infinite number there and almost all died. In sum I say that where the Spaniards planted their flag they unleashed the greatest cruelty, and it became a sign of perpetual hate to the indigenous.

---

the mortality caused by foreign diseases like smallpox. Crosby, *Columbian Exchange*, 45; Cook, *Born to Die*, 25.

And now to touch on religion. Not only in this island, but also in all the other nations of this new world, they worshipped, and still worship, many different gods. Some they have painted, some they have as statues, some in clay, others in wood, some in gold and some in silver. In certain places, especially in the Kingdom of Peru, I have seen them in the form of birds, tigers, deer, and other sorts of animals. Most I have seen are made with a tail down to the feet, like our Satan. Still our priests and friars take them every day and destroy them whenever possible. But the priests of their religion still have many of them hidden in caves underground. They sacrifice to them secretly, continuously asking them how they might expel the Christians from their land.

They have appointed each one by name as the advocate over one thing or another like the ancients used to do in the old days. Then you had Mars in charge of victories on earth, and in the sea it was Neptune. Asclepius had medicine. Hercules presided over good weather, with people promising him a tenth of their property if he would take care of it and make it prosper. These people do not ask anything of their gods except for an abundance of food and drink, good health, and victory over their enemies. Many times the devil appears in various and different forms, promising the priests various wishes, and not following through on his promises. He does not follow through and they complain, and he responds that he changed his mind because they committed some grievous sin. And with this the father of lies excuses himself.

When a lord of the island of Hispaniola wanted to celebrate the festival of his primary and false god, he commanded all of his vassals, both men and women, to come to a usual location and get in line. The lord went inside the temple where the priests were preparing the idols. There he proceeded to play the drums. All the other people followed him inside. The men were painted black, red, and yellow, and wore plumes made of feathers of parrots and other sacred birds. They also wore bands of seashells around their necks, legs, and arms. The women came in without paint. The girls were completely naked and the married women covered their shameful parts, as on the Gulf of Paria and other parts of the mainland. They entered the temple like this and danced and sang certain songs praising the idols. The lord greeted them with his drum. Then they vomited by shoving a stick down their throat so the idols could see that they had nothing impure in their stomachs and chest.

After doing these crazy rituals, they all sat down on their heels and sang some other songs with a melancholic tone. Then some other women entered the temple carrying a chest decorated with roses and other flowers and full of bread. They went around to the others in turn and sang certain prayers. The others jumped to their feet to answer, and when they finished these songs they sang others dedicated to their lords, about their glory and honor. Then they presented the bread to the idols. The priests then took the bread and blessed it and passed it around to all the people as if it were a holy or blessed relic. And so everyone, very joyful and content, returned home.

They believe that the sun and moon came from a cave.[33] They had a pumpkin for a relic; they said that it had come from the sea with the fish. They had two wooden statues that they worshipped as the gods of abundance. At certain times during the year, many Indians went on pilgrimage. They also had an idol with four feet like a dog and they said that when it was angry it went into the mountains. They had to go retrieve it and bring it back to the temple on their shoulders.

In this island, as in some other provinces of this new land, there were many saplings, not too big, like reeds, that produced a leaf shaped like a walnut leaf, but bigger. It is held in great esteem by the Indians and by the slaves the Spaniards brought from Ethiopia. When these leaves are in season, they pick them, tie them up in bundles, and suspend them near their fireplace until they are very dry. When they want to use them, they get a leaf of their grain and put these leaves inside it and roll them together like a cannon. Then they light one end and put the other in their mouths and breathe through it. The smoke goes into their mouth, head, and throat, as long as they can take it, because it brings them pleasure. And they fill themselves with this cruel smoke until they lose reason. Some take so much of it they fall down as if they were dead and stay there for the better part of the day or night. Others are happy to just sip the smoke so their head gets turned around, and that is enough. See what a troublesome and dangerous weed from the devil this is! It has happened to me many times that traveling around the provinces of Guatemala and Nicaragua, I entered the house of some Indians who had just taken

---

33. The Taíno believed that the gods of the sun and the rain emerged from a cave. Martin-Fragachan, "Cultures in the New World," 276.

some of this herb, which in the Mexican language they call tobacco,[34] [and] that immediately after smelling its acute and fetid stench, I was forced to leave and go somewhere else.

In the island of Hispaniola and in all the other islands, when their doctors wanted to cure a sick man they went to a place to administer smoke.[35] When the patient was completely intoxicated, the cure was almost done. After he returned to his senses, he told a thousand stories, of having seen the council of the gods and other exalted visions. Then they turned the sick man around three or four times and they rubbed his back with their hands, making faces, and holding a piece of bone or stone in their mouths. These are things the women hold as sacred, believing that these tokens will ease childbirth.

If the sick man asks the doctor what will happen to him, the doctor responds that he will soon become free. If he dies, the doctor has many excuses, but the best is that he was mortal. And if any doctor visits a patient without having done the usual rituals, he is severely punished. In many provinces I visited, I often heard that the doctors were also the priests, so it was probably like that everywhere. In their language, they call them *bocchiti*, and in every place they have great authority.[36] They don't do medicine on most people, only on the most powerful.

Everyone takes as many wives as they want. One is held as the principal wife and she commands the others. When a lord dies without heirs, he is succeeded by his nephews—the sons of his sisters— and not by his brothers. They have more certainty that the boys are her sons than those of doubtful parentage. The reason is because very few in these countries have chastity, and in few places do they bother to guard their daughters and sisters. All sleep together like chickens, some on the ground, and some suspended in the air. When the

---

34. It is unclear what this plant actually was. The word *tobacco* probably comes from a Taíno word for "rolled tobacco leaves," but that could cover a number of varieties, some stronger than others. See Gray, *History of Agriculture*, 1:21, 218, 769–70, 886. In fact, this passage reads more like a description of marijuana use. *Cannabis sativa* was first cultivated in the eastern steppes of Asia and made its way to the Americas intentionally via traders and less methodically via slaves from Africa. Barney Warf, "High Points," 418, 423–25. It is unlikely that Benzoni would have understood this, and he might well have used the word for tobacco to describe any plants smoked recreationally, including one that would make the user "lose reason." The Mexican (Nahuatl) word for tobacco is *iyetl*.

35. Winter, *Tobacco Use by Native North Americans*, 56–57.

36. Probably *behique*, another type of indigenous shaman.

Modo che tengono i medici nel medicare gl'infermi.

FIG. 5 How doctors care for the sick. "Modo che tengono i medici nel medicare gl'infermi." In Benzoni, *La historia del Mondo Nuovo*, 1565. Courtesy of the John Carter Brown Library at Brown University.

women give birth, they carry the baby to the seashore or to a river to wash them. Without any other preparation, they nurse them.

Some say that they were great thieves and for every little thing their law commands that they be killed. But what would they steal? They are not greedy for riches. Whatever gold or silver they might lack and want they can go to the mine and procure as if it were water at a fountain. As for clothing, they all go naked. As for food, they all give to whomever comes to their house. During their festivals they all relax together, everyone bringing things to eat and drink, and they sing and dance until everyone gets drunk and tired. They freely have a good time. So I can't imagine that they would steal, which is against their nature, unless they had already learned to steal from the first, or second, or third Spaniard who had begun to live with them. Would to the Omnipotent God that we would be more like them in regard to temporal riches. The name Christian would be heavenly should they rid themselves of avarice.

These people call their grain *maize* in their language. It comes from the island of Hispaniola, the first found by the Christians. The wine is *chicha*, boats are *canoue*, swords are *macanne*, and the lords are called *caciques*.[37] They don't work the earth to grow their grain. They just poke a little hole and drop three or four seeds in, then cover it back up. That suffices. Each stalk produces three or four ears of 100 grains each. The stalks of corn are taller than a man and in many provinces they are able to harvest them two times a year.

The women who mix the grain are called *molandaie*. They take a bit of this grain and wet it thoroughly with some cold water in the evening. In the morning they slowly break it into pieces with two stones. Some do it while standing and some do it on their knees in the earth. They don't care if hair or lice goes in. They make the dough with wet hands and shape them into little breads, some long, some round. They put them in reed leaves with as little water as possible. Then they cook them. This is the bread of commoners. It lasts two days and then it mildews.

The lords eat like this: they mash it with two stones and wash it with hot water, picking out the husks, leaving only the flour. They grind that as much as possible and then shape them into little round cakes. They cook those in round pans in the oven, slowly increasing the fire. The women take great pains with this bread and it must be eaten fresh because it is not good if it is well done or cold. It is good if it is just right: warm, not hot and not cold. I've gone into uninhabited countries and, with need as my guide, learned to mix this so I wouldn't have to eat raw or roasted maize. Grinding it is hard and it wore me out. Many times, since I had only a little bit, I didn't pick out the husks like the lords. Nor did grinding it fine suit my arms, destroyed and disabled by hunger as they were.

---

37. Most of these words come from Taíno or Arawak, languages spoken in the Caribbean islands. The outlier is *chicha*, which comes from Kuna, a language spoken in the region between Panama and Colombia.

Modo di fare il pane.

FIG. 6 How to make bread. "Modo di fare il pane." In Benzoni, *La historia del Mondo Nuovo*, 1565. Courtesy of the John Carter Brown Library at Brown University.

They have another kind of bread they call *cabazi*,[38] made from a root called *yucca*, which is about the size of a parsnip. This root does not produce any seeds at all, except some gnarled reeds. The leaves are green like the leaves of hemp. When this plant is in season, they cut it in pieces about two palms long and plant it in big piles of dirt called *conuchi*.[39] After two years, they have big roots. Every time they want to make this bread they uncover them—but only a little at a time or they spoil—and they peel and cut them with sharp

38. I.e., cassava, *caçabi* in Taíno.
39. Benzoni's description of agriculture and labor is an accurate depiction of Carib practice. Whitehead, *Lords of the Tiger Spirit*, 51.

stones that they find on the beach. They put them into a funnel, then squeeze out the juice. The result is poisonous to anyone who drinks it. They lay this out like *focaccia* on a large rock and cook it over the fire as long as it can hold together.[40] After it is done, they put the loaves in the sun to dry. They make some thick and some thin. This bread seems to me really disgusting, but if you put it in a dry place it will last two, maybe three, years. You have to drink something to wet your throat when you eat it so you can swallow it. I thought it tasted like eating dirt. With a bit of beef broth it is better, but not much. All the ships that return to Spain (except those from Veracruz) lay in stores of this bread for the trips back. They do this because there is not a single grain of wheat in all the lands, places, islands, and provinces of this new land inhabited by Spaniards. Anyone who has wheat or biscuits got them from Mexico through a journey of over two hundred miles via mules and carts.

There are also two other kinds of roots, one called *battata* and the other called *haie,* they are of the same shape, except *haie* is smaller and tastes better than the other.[41] Six months after they are planted, they bear fruit. Their flavor is pretty sweet, but you quickly get tired of it, and then there is little substance in them. Usually they are cooked in the embers of the fire. When you eat them, they give you gas. Some people say they taste like marzipan or sweetened walnuts, but according to me, even unsweetened chestnuts are better.

Since I've told you about making bread I should tell you about wine, too, especially about the kind they make with corn. The *molandaie* gather a quantity of the grain that seems about right for making the amount of wine they want to make. After having mixed it, they put it in some large jars with water. The women who are in charge of making this beverage mix it a little in a cooking pot. Then they hand it over to other women whose job it is to put it in their mouths and chew it, bit by bit. Then they spit it out very forcefully onto a leaf, before putting all of this back in the pot. If they don't do this, then the wine will have no strength. Then they boil it for three or four hours, then take it off the fire and let it cool. After that, they strain it through a cloth and leave it until it reaches the right strength. Then they drink it and get drunk, just as if they drank real wine.

40. *Focaccia* is an Italian flat bread.
41. *Batata* and *age* are Taíno words for two kinds of sweet potatoes.

Modo di fare il uino.

FIG. 7 How to make wine. "Modo di fare il uino." In Benzoni, *La historia del Mondo Nuovo*, 1565. Courtesy of the John Carter Brown Library at Brown University.

They also make other kinds of wine, from honey, fruit, and roots, but they aren't intoxicating like the others. They have a great quantity of trees that produce a sort of wild grape. Its fruit is like blackthorn, the black berries that grow among the thorns and have black skins. But because the pits are large and there isn't much skin, they don't make wine out of them. There are some trees that produce olives, but with a terrible smell and worse flavor. They have an abundance of different kinds of fruits, *houi,* plantains, pines, guavas, mammee apples, and guanábana. The *houi* are canary plums. They have little meat and a large stone and are yellow when they are ripe. Its tree is large and the leaves are small, with a sour flavor.

A plantain is a fruit that is longer than it is wide. The smaller ones are better than the large ones. Its tree has leaves that are one and

a half palms wide and four and a half palms long. A branch grows
between the leaves. It produces one hundred or more little plantains
and twenty-five or more of the big ones. This tree is tender and only
bears fruit once a year. Other plants grow from the roots. If the fruit
is ripe they pick it, but if it is green, they cut down the tree and put
it in a hot place so it can ripen quickly and turn yellow. The skin is
thick as the blade of a knife and the rest is pulp. Its taste leans toward
sweet. The pineapples grow in bushes and when they are mature
they turn yellow. They have a nice odor and a better flavor. They are
colorful. And sometimes when I am sick I can't eat anything else but
this fruit. To my taste, I believe that this is one of the most appetizing
fruits in the world. After removing the skin, the rest is all meat. Generally it is of a sweet flavor, with a bit of sour. The guava is a tree-
like peach with leaves like a laurel but bigger and longer. It matures
quickly. Its fruit is like the medlar but much larger. It ripens on the
tree and if it isn't picked when ripe it produces worms. It has many
small seeds inside. The red taste better than the white.

In all of these above-mentioned islands there were no quadrupeds
whatsoever except for some small rabbits. There were certain pests
named *nati nigue*,[42] about as big as fleas. They can wiggle themselves
between the finger and the nail, often without anyone feeling it,
especially in the feet, until they grow to about the size of a bean.
Then they have to be pulled out with a needle or a thorn. The wound
is cleaned and healed with hot ashes. Many black slaves get so many
of them in their feet, since they go barefoot, that there is nothing
to do except to drive them out with a hot iron. Many people have
been left crippled because of this. This happened to me, too, in Peru,
in the province of Puerto Viejo. I got so tired from my travels across
the sea and land that I was covered by an itchy rash on my body and
my legs. I got so many *nigue* on my feet that I got scared. If I hadn't
been so careful to keep myself clean and went so often to the river
to wash myself, many bad things would have happened to me. Many
Spaniards, maybe through laziness, refused to wash themselves two
or three times a day and then ended up lame for life.

I have already said how the island of Haiti (named Hispaniola
by Admiral Columbus) is 1,200 miles in circumference.[43] It has an

---

42. The sand flea, *Tunga penetrans*, which burrows into skin to lay its eggs.

43. The name Haiti comes from the Taíno word *ayiti*, meaning "land of high
mountains." For most of the colonial period, the island was known as Hispaniola. Only

abundance of ports, rivers, fish, and salt. There are two lakes, one salt and the other fresh. The richest river of gold the Spaniards found in this island is called Cibao, and the principal city is called Santo Domingo. It was built by Bartolomé Colón, who gave it that name because he was going around the island, looking for a good port that was commodious for his ships arriving from Spain, and came upon that location on the day of Santo Domingo.[44] The town is built on a plain by the water and in my time it was made up of about five hundred hearths. The houses are nice, like those in Spain. On the west side the river Ozonca descends and empties into the sea to a good and safe port that is large enough for many ships. There are huge, thick woods. The island is 220 miles wide and 600 miles long (skipping a bit about the poles).[45]

Some say that wheat grows well in this island because of the strength of the soil, but they don't grow much there because there is an abundance of maize. But I say that they gather neither a lot, nor even a little. I asked a few old Spaniards why and they told me that the land was too hot to produce it, as it is in all the islands. It is true that at first, when people first started to live in these islands, a few Spanish peasants planted a little bit in some mountains near Cibao, which is cool enough, and they harvested about two *stara*.[46] But the mountains were harsh and rocky and the peasants quickly saw that they would not be able to grow very much there, so they stopped planting it. And so they get their wheat delivered in casks from Spain. When they cannot find bread because the ships are late, they have to eat squash because they don't grow much maize there because of this grain.

Only a few of the trees brought from Spain grow well. Only pomegranates, oranges, cedars, lemons, and certain figs. Vines produce only very small bunches of grapes, so they earn only one half a ducat per pound. And I saw a vineyard owned by Secretary Diego Caballero that had several thousand vines, but it was a good year when he harvested even forty pounds of grapes. They don't have a very good

---

after the Haitian Revolution (1791–1804) did the formerly French colony of Saint-Domingue (the western half of the island) adopt the older name of Haiti.

44. The city of Santo Domingo was founded in 1496.

45. Here Benzoni uses the measure of a *miglio* (mile), a difficult measure to convert because it varied over time and between Italian regions.

46. Probably the Spanish *fanega*, or bushel, a volume equivalent to roughly fifty-five liters.

flavor and generally harvest in February and March. Summer begins in January and lasts until the end of April. Winter begins in May and finishes in December. It is not called winter because it is cold, but because of the abundance of rain; in fact it is hotter than summer because the winds stop and hot and humid vapors rise from the earth and generate many illnesses. On the other hand, in the summer the winds come from the east and northeast and the skies are clear.

Among the things from the garden there are cabbages, radishes, lettuce, pumpkins, and melon in abundance. Onions and garlic rarely do well. Ships from Spain bring them in great quantities with many other things, like beans, chickpeas, lentils, almonds, walnuts, figs, raisins, oil, rice, apples, cheese, jugs, plates, bowls, spices, cloth, silk, leather, wine, biscuits, and other things that cannot be found.

There is a great number of every sort of variety of livestock found in Spain. There are some Spaniards who have six or eight thousand head of cattle in that country. Everyone can kill for their own use whatever they would like as long as they give the hide to the owner. In this island there is also a large amount of sugar and in my time thirty-four mills were working. So these two things—sugar and leather—are the principal market goods of this island, and the merchants who are presently arriving from Spain do not take anything else when they return because the Spaniards have so stripped the metal, yellow and white, that not even a grain can be found. The largest coin minted in Santo Domingo is worth four *maravedis*, which is one of our *soldi*.[47] And if merchants wish to buy gold or silver (because some from Peru or Cabo Fondura is still carried by the merchants who come to buy horses, slaves, and mules), you might be able to do it, but at a loss, because one ducat of good gold is worth two of other coins. Because of this they buy leather, sugar, *cassia*, and *guaiacavo*, which is holy wood.

End of the First Book

---

47. In the late fifteenth century, the smallest, lowest-denomination coins were minted in multiples of four, eight, or sixteen *maravedis*. By the mid-sixteenth century, *maravedis* had become a unit of accounting and were no longer minted. Various Spanish coins were valued in *maravedis* in order to account for the different weight and purity of the gold and silver used. This system also allowed for easy conversion between silver and gold coins, as each had its own value in *maravedis*. Schwaller, *Origins of Church Wealth*, 5.

Book II

At the time that the Indians of this island had begun their decline into ultimate ruin, the Spaniards brought over a great number of Moors from Guinea,[1] which was a conquest of the king of Portugal.[2] Back when there were mines, they worked there with gold and silver, but those ran dry.[3] After that, the Spaniards increased the number of sugar plantations, so now many Moors work in these, and as shepherds, and do anything else to please their masters.

You find among the Spaniards not just cruel people, but indeed the very cruelest of people. They want to punish a slave for whatever misdeed he has committed, such as for not having earned enough for the day, or for some mischief he might have done, or for not having brought up enough silver or gold from the mine. When he comes home in the evening, instead of feeding him dinner, they make him undress (if he happened to be wearing a shirt), throw him down on the ground, and tie his hands and feet across a piece of wood. Among the Spaniards this is called the law of Bayona.[4] This law, I believe, was

1. By the sixteenth century, Spanish speakers had begun to refer to sub-Saharan Africans as *negros*. Benzoni's use of *Moro* suggests that Italians had not yet begun to refer to such people solely on the basis of their skin color.

2. Portuguese expansion along the African coast was often described as "conquest," despite the fact that it primarily involved the establishment of trading posts, not colonies. The conquests to which Benzoni alludes here were chronicled in Eannes de Azurara, *Descobrimento e conquista de Guiné*.

3. In the Circum-Caribbean, placer mining for gold along riverbeds was most common. Higman, *Concise History of the Caribbean*, 65.

4. The Estatuto de Bayona referred to a set of practices used by masters to punish slaves. This description seems to include an assortment of punishments that may not have been used together. For another example, see Villa-Flores, "'To Lose One's Soul,'" 444.

written by some great demon. Then, with a strap or a piece of rope, they beat him until blood streams from his body. When it is over, they cook a pound of pitch or a little bit of boiling oil and, little by little, put it over his whole body. He then washes with water, some salt, and the pepper of that country. Then they cover him and leave him lying on the table until the master deems him ready to return to work. Others dig a hole in the ground and put him in it, covering him completely until only his head sticks out, and leave him there all night. The Spaniards say they do this because the ground absorbs the blood and protects the flesh so it will not develop sores and he will get well sooner. If someone dies (as sometimes happens), the penalty for this great sin, according to the law of the Spaniards, is just that they must get a new slave for the king.

Because of this great cruelty, many of the slaves in this territory began to run away from their masters and wandered lost around the island. But they have multiplied to such numbers that they have given, and continue to give, the Spaniards who live there a lot of trouble. The kings of Ethiopia, the Quinei, Manicongri, Gialopi, Zapi, Berbersi, are always at war with one another, and take one another prisoner and then sell one another to the Portuguese.[5] So in this country they still bear one another some hatred, but they do not mistreat one another. On the contrary, because of the assaults of the Spaniards, they give one another help and favor. Each nation recognizes its own king or governor and keeps itself separate from the others.[6] Because of this, they do not do the harm to the Spaniards that they could if they would unite.[7]

Seeing that every day the number of these Moors multiplied, and that all the Spaniards that fell into their hands were killed after all manner of torments, the presidents and leaders of the islands began to gather men and send them to all the parts of the island where the

5. Although the Portuguese did do some slave raiding, especially early in their expansion along Africa's coast, most slaves sold to the Americas were enslaved by rival African groups. Thornton, *Africa and Africans*, 72–125.
6. In the Americas, Africans frequently tried to maintain ethnic and kinship ties and occasionally organized themselves by "nation," electing leaders whom they often labeled kings. Ibid., 202–5.
7. In some African slave rebellions, ethnic solidarity appears to have strengthened resistance movements. In 1537 and 1612, the election of an African king by slaves in Mexico led to brutal repression by Spanish authorities fearful that slaves were plotting revolt. Martínez, "Black Blood of New Spain."

Moors live.[8] At first, these raids went well for the Spaniards because
they promised freedom to some Moors who knew the areas where
they lived and led the Spaniards there to attack at night. Like beasts,
the Moors slept without any fear of their enemies and the Spaniards
were able to kill many of them. But then the Moors began to keep
watch, and were very vigilant, and almost always the Spaniards got
the worst of it. And so these proud men have multiplied to such a
great number that when I lived there it was said with certainty that
there were over 7,000. In the year '45, when I was on the island,
I heard that the *Cimarrónes* (because this is what the Spaniards call
them) in this country had joined in rebellion the general exiles who
scoured the island, going all over and making all sorts of mischief
they could manage.[9] It was so bad that Admiral Don Luis Colón, and
the president, and the leaders of Santo Domingo send messengers
to beg and pray that the Moors be content to live in peace.[10] The
Spaniards promised to do the same, that they would not bother them
again and that they wanted to be friends. If the Moors wanted priests
or friars to teach them the doctrine of Christ, the Spaniards would be
most willing to send them out. To this the rebels responded that they
believed in the laws of Christ but that they did not want their friendship because they did not trust their promises.

There are many Spaniards who believe for certain that this island
will, in a very short time, fall into the hands of these Moors. And
because of that, the governors remain very vigilant. When any ships
want to leave for another province in the Indies, the Spaniards will
not let them go without their permission, even if they are merchants.

8. The chief justice of the Audiencia held the title of president. Despite being
a court, the Audiencia exercised some legislative authority in conjunction with the
governor.

9. The term *cimarrón* has a disputed etymology. It may come from a Spanish
conjunction of *cima* (top) and *marrón* (brown), implying the brown men that inhabit
the hilltops or high places. Conversely, it may be derived from a Taíno word for an
arrow that has been shot, implying something gone astray or wild. In addition to runaway slaves, *cimarrón* could also describe feral livestock. Guillot, *Negros rebeldes y
negros cimarrones*, 38; Arrom, "Cimarrón," 56–57.

10. Spanish policy against runaway slaves varied according to circumstances.
Isolated groups were often ignored if they did not harass Spanish interests. Larger
communities that endangered Spanish commerce, trade, or industry faced military
campaigns. If these failed, the Spanish used negotiation in order to restore peace, even
if that involved pardoning and freeing runaway slaves. Altman, "Revolt of Enriquillo,"
611–14; Pike, "Black Rebels."

However, when the licentiate Cerrato was president of this island, he brought a provision of liberty to the Indians, and opened travel to all, allowing everyone to go where they pleased.[11] For this he was criticized by some citizens, and he replied, "After his Majesty the Emperor had given the Indians freedom, it did not seem fair to me that the Spaniards ought, contrary to the will of his Majesty, to be held as slaves. I just follow his precedent, and it seems to me to be fair that the people might go freely wherever they please." But then he learned just how much the island was becoming uninhabited, and that there were very few Spaniards left—not more than 1,100— while the outlaws were growing stronger daily. When he learned this news, that there were not enough Spaniards to defend themselves and that they were in danger of losing the island and their lives, he became very concerned and closed the port. So, among the Spaniards who go adventuring in the Indies and visit this island, there are few who want to stay there, because everyone passes through these countries to get rich and in this island that is not possible.

Since I mentioned several things that happened in this island between the Moors and the Spaniards, I should also tell you about the incredible damage inflicted by the French in these Indies, by sea and by land, to the Spanish nation. Not long after these islands were found, many French corsairs heard about great riches and began to travel around the sea during the war, looking for ships that came from the Indies. They took a lot of them. Among the other riches they stole, one time they took a ship that was carrying the great and inestimable riches of Peru; there was so much on it that the share for every one of the ship's men was 800 gold ducats.[12]

The main reason the French took so many ships from the Spaniards was the avarice of their Spanish owners. When they left from Spain, the owners of the ships were so intent on filling the ship with merchandise and passengers that they did not take care to bring artillery with them in case they needed to defend themselves against enemy ships. They did not even carry what was ordered by the Council of the Indies, which commanded that each ship carry at least

11. Alonso López de Cerrato served as the president of the Audiencia of Santo Domingo. By "liberty" granted to the Indians, Benzoni means the promulgation of the New Laws of 1542.

12. Probably the pirate attack of Jean Florin in 1523; Florin and his men captured more than sixty-two thousand gold ducats. Lane, *Pillaging the Empire*, 18.

two bronze guns and six large guns made of iron, and other small guns, several barrels of powder, and other weapons. The Council appointed several commissioners with special power to go to Sanlúcar to visit the ships as they were about to embark to see if they were provisioned according to the rules set out by the Council. But the owners of these vessels put a few pieces of gold in the hands of these commissioners and they will say that everything is fine. And with this blessing they go to their superiors in Seville in the House of Trade,[13] and swore to God that everything was perfectly in order and that every ship was capable of fighting four French vessels. And this is how approximately three or four Spanish ships used to set out carrying at best two or three pieces of iron artillery, half eaten out with rust, and one barrel of not very good powder. Then, if a well-armed little French galleon[14] ran into the Spaniards, it would attack a ship that weighed 1,500 or 2,000 *salme* without any fear because they already knew they were poorly outfitted.[15] They first tossed a few shots over the top, then demanded they lower the mainsail for the king of France. If the Spaniards took too long to lower the sails, they shot large artillery directly amidships. The Spaniards saw right away that there was no way they could defend themselves, and fearing that everyone would die, they surrendered. The Frenchmen immediately demanded that the captain lower a boat and come to their ship along with the pilot and a clerk. And so they demanded a list of the gold, silver, pearls, and other things of value they usually carried home. Then the French took everything and they allowed their men to go onto the ships and see if they could find anything else. As soon as they got on board, they stripped the passengers and sailors. If any of the Spaniards were well dressed, the Frenchmen exchanged their rags for the Spaniards' clothes, saying, "This is good for you, and this is for me." Neither respect for the power of Spain nor rules of war restrained them from tearing apart the rooms, looking in every nook and cranny for a spare piece of gold. Some captains were content to just take the booty and leave the ships. But most of them carried the ships to France, putting the sailors to shore with a handful of coins

13. The Casa de Contración, the government agency charged with overseeing maritime commerce.

14. Benzoni calls them *galleoncetti*.

15. A *salma* is an old unit of measurement equaling sixty-four imperial gallons. These ships would weigh three to four hundred tons.

to get them home. Of all the captains, pilots, and clerks who traded in the Indies, only a few were not taken to France one or two times.

After I was in Hispaniola for eleven months, I left the city of Santo Domingo for the mainland on a boat.[16] At the end of six days, we arrived within sight of the snowy mountains of Santa Marta. We quickly entered into the city of Cartagena. It is called that because it has an island at the mouth of the port, like the city of Cartagena in Spain. This island is eight miles in length and three in width. When the Spaniards first arrived in this country, it was completely inhabited by Indian fishermen, but now there is not even a sign of the houses that were there.[17] We need not be even a little surprised by this, since in every province the Spanish have crossed, either on land or on water, it is hard to find even a few miserable Indian villages. This great damage was done because when there was even the smallest bit of fight left in the people, they would not accept the friendship of the Spaniards because of the cruelties used among them. They have an abundance of fruit, fish, and all the other things necessary to sustain life. They cover their shameful parts with bands of cotton. When they go to war, the women fight as well as the men. Their arms are poisoned arrows; they eat their enemies—and they have eaten many Spaniards and would do the same to the others if they could.

When they have holidays, they dress themselves as well as possible, with jewelry of gold, pearls, and emeralds. They put them on their arms, their faces, and on other parts of their bodies. Their principal goods are salt, fish, and pepper. They carry these inland where they need them, and barter for other things. In times of prosperity, they had large and beautiful markets of grain, fruit, cotton, feathers, jewelry, gold, different sorts of pearls, emeralds, slaves, and other things. They took only what they needed, without avarice, saying you take this and give me that other thing. The thing they value the most, among all items, are things to eat. But now most of them have learned from us to hold temporal goods in the highest esteem.

16.   Here we have cut a long passage about the ongoing war between the French and the Spaniards in the Caribbean and at home in Europe.

17.   The lack of pre-Columbian housing is not surprising. The city of Cartagena de Indias was founded on the site of a conquered indigenous community called Calamar. The new city would have destroyed the preexisting structures, while contagious disease decimated the population of the surrounding hinterland. Del Castillo Mathieu, *Descubrimiento y conquista de Colombia*, 72–73.

Still, there are some who do not value these things, as they did before. This happened to me when I went to an Indian's house and asked if he had a chicken to sell me. He answered me like this: what do you want to give me in exchange? I showed him a *real*. He took it from my hand, saying to me: "What do you want to do with the chicken?" And I responded that I wanted to eat it. The Indian looked me in the eye, put the coin between his teeth, and said: "O, Christian, if you want me to give you something to eat, you give me a proper exchange, something that I can also eat. Because what you are offering me is worth nothing at all. Take your *real* and give me my chicken."[18] And so I went to someone else's house and he gave me a chicken.

This province was named New Granada.[19] Captain Jorge Robledo built the city of Cartagena in the year 1540 and gave it this name because nearly all the conquistadors who were there when he arrived were from Cartagena in Spain.[20] From there they excavated, and still excavate, a great quantity of emeralds.

The Velzare also heard about this very rich find.[21] They left Venezuela immediately by land for the open land. They crossed the snowy mountains of Santa Marta with good Indian guides, and walked all the way until they arrived at the province of the emeralds. After making a few forays and destroying some Indians, they returned to their territory. With this, these Indians saw themselves oppressed on all sides by strange people and unable to handle the pain. And so, abusing, condemning, and denouncing the name Christian, they used to go out to the woods and hang themselves. And so the women went just like the men. Because most of them go nude, they had nothing to tie themselves up with. So they help one another by tying their hair to the branches of the trees and then letting themselves fall. With most horrible laments, full of pain with screams and shrieks, they filled the air with their miseries, and let themselves die.

18. A *real* was one-eighth of a peso, hence the English term "piece of eight" for Spanish pesos. Although local prices could vary wildly depending on the availability of gold and silver coins, a *real* had significant purchasing power. In the sixteenth century, an unskilled laborer earned a *real* for a full day's work. Gibson, *Aztecs Under Spanish Rule*, 250–51.

19. Here we have excised a passage about Spaniards seeking emeralds.

20. Benzoni has conflated two cities and their founders. In 1533, Don Pedro de Heredia founded the city of Cartagena on the coast. In 1540, Jorge Robledo founded the city of Cartago in the interior.

21. Welsers were a German banking family. In 1528, Charles V had granted them rights to settle and explore Venezuela.

The inhabitants of the valley of Tunja and other nearby places hold the sun as their principal god.[22] When they go to war, they carry the bones of famous warriors attached to canes above their heads instead of a standard so the others will be moved to imitate their valor, and so they battle ardently against their enemies. Their arms are lances made of palm trees with flint stones. They bury their lords with their jewelry of gold and emeralds, and bread and wine; the Spaniards found many rich tombs. The inhabitants who live on the banks of the big river are Caribs, like those from Santa Marta. They have arrows tinted with herbs. Before the Spaniards entered the territory, they were the principal enemy of the Bogotá; they always warred against one another.[23] They are brave, fierce, and vindictive, and when they go to war, they carry with them their god Chiappe, the god of victory.[24] Before they leave, they offer multiple sacrifices, killing some children of some slave, or someone taken from their enemies, smearing their blood all over them and eating their flesh together. If they find themselves victorious, they do the same with the blood of their enemies drawn in battle. Then, with great joy they sing, dance, and get drunk. But if they are defeated, they are sad, moody, and sorrowful, offering the idol new sacrifices to placate him so he will be better to them and give them victory.

There are many other things that could be said about these provinces and their customs, but so as to not to be boring I will go on. Turning again to my voyage: in Cartagena, the boat I was in took in a lot of water so it was not able to leave right away and had to wait for another passage. At the end of forty-four days, I embarked in a brigantine that was going to Nombre de Dios. We always kept to the coast, so we entered into the Gulf of Uraba, and then the port of the city of Acla, which was just two bow shots from shore. There were about eight houses inhabited by Spaniards. There were more when the city was first built, but things have been going, and continue to go, downhill.[25]

---

22.   The Valley of Tunja was inhabited by the Muisca civilization. The Muisca were polytheists; their sun deity was named Bohica. Izard, *Tierra firme*, 36–37.

23.   Here, Bogotá refers to a Muisca community, Bacatá. By the time of the Spanish conquest (1537), Bacatá had become a regional power. Trimborn, "Organización del poder público"; Gamboa Mendoza, *Cacicazgo muisca*, 35–45.

24.   It is unclear what deity is being described here.

25.   The city of Acla was founded in 1515 but was completely abandoned by the mid-1530s. Conflicts with neighboring indigenous groups and runaway slaves severely weakened the community.

So for them, like the Indians, the better part of them went to find better fortunes. The same happened at [Santa María la] Antigua [del] Darién and the other locations on this coast.[26]

Eight days before I arrived at the port of Acla, a ship arrived from Santo Domingo full of mules bound for Nombre de Dios. But on reaching the mainland, the pilot, not knowing the coast and being certain that he was actually lower in the terminus of Veragua, turned the ship, expecting to get to Nombre de Dios. But instead he was heading to Cartagena, tacking down the coast, until he got to the mouth of this port. The pilot did not know where he was or where he was going, so he just sat there, uncertain, looking at the land. Then a Spaniard, taking a walk on the shore, saw that the ship at the mouth of the port was not coming in. He believed that the ship wasn't coming in because it didn't know the landscape. So he immediately ran home, got a piece of white cloth that he tied on a lance, and returned to the shore.

When they saw the signal, the people on the ship entered into the port and unloaded the mules. The merchants thought that if they turned around and reloaded the mules they might die from the stress. They decided to send the ship to Nombre de Dios and to lead the mules overland to Panama [City]. And so they began to get things in order, foraging for adequate provisions to sustain them for the trip. The merchants asked if I would like to come in their company, and so we left, led by a not too experienced Spaniard as a guide and twenty Moorish slaves who belonged to the merchants. Each of them carried a blade in his hand for opening up the road. Without this, we would never have been able to go forward because the road was blocked by stinging branches.

After having walked very slowly for fourteen days, when we still had made it only about halfway, we saw the ruins of the habitation of many people from the time of their prosperity. The merchants had already proposed we kill a mule, because the provisions had run out, when one evening at sunset, while standing on the summit of a hill— to everyone's great joy—we saw a large plume of smoke. The guide told us that it was the residence of some Indians, but that it seemed to him that we should wait to go until three or four in the morning

26. The port city of Nombre de Dios and its easier overland connections to Panama City contributed to the abandonment of Acla and Antigua. Mena García, *Sociedad de Panamá*, 48, 78.

and take them by surprise. He surmised that this made sense because
if they saw us they would think that we were coming to capture
them for slaves (as was the custom among the Spaniards before the
imperial guarantee of their freedom),[27] and they would flee into the
forest and we would get no provisions.

And so we did it like that. To make sure that we would not be
seen, we climbed halfway down the mountain and waited most
of the night. Then we went to the hamlet where there were four
small houses. We went in. The Indians, hearing the noise, woke up,
and as they became aware of our presence they started to scream,
"Guacci! Guacci!" The word sounds like that and it signifies a small,
four-legged nocturnal predator, and is the name they have given
the Christians. Then we went into the huts and seized all the people
inside them, and kept watch for the rest of the night. I can say that
I have never heard such crying, especially from the women, as I did
that night, because they were certain that we had come to take them
for slaves. They let their heads sag dejectedly, lamented among themselves, smashed their heads into the ground, and tore at our clothes
with their hands and their teeth like wild beasts. They spat in our
faces. Really, if we had not prevented them, some of them would have
killed themselves.

It was so bad that when dawn broke, and they stopped some of
their terrifying screams, we tried our best to placate them. With
signs we tried to make them understand that we had not come for
any reason other than to get something to eat so we could pass with
our mules to the other sea, and that they did not have to have any
further fear because the king of Castile had commanded that slaves
should no longer be taken. So with these words, and some others we
said, they began to calm a little but they were still afraid of some
treachery.

This is how we were supplied with bread, fish, fruit, and the meat
of wild boar—which in the Indies generally have bristles down their
backs.[28] For payment we offered them a few knives and some salt.
We wanted to leave them some *reals*, but they did not want to take

27.   The decree of freedom was included as part of the New Laws of 1542.
28.   Probably the peccary, also known as a *javelina,* but possibly Eurasian pigs that
had gone feral in the Americas. Within a few generations, the physical appearance of
feral Eurasian hogs mirrored that of wild boar, for example, the razorback of the south-
eastern United States. Crosby, *Columbian Exchange,* 77.

them, saying that they did not know what to do with them. After we
rested for four days, we left, and one Indian decided to come with us
for quite a ways until he got us on the right path. We asked him if
there were some other Indian villages on the road and he responded
that there were not because the Guacci had seized and killed the
Indians and destroyed the entire country. And with that the Indian
returned home. After eight days we reached Panama, completely
exhausted.

Some say that the features of this city are almost as great as those
of Venice. But I believe that these authors cannot have seen the more
magnificent and illustrious city of Venice. That city is of such exalted
height, not just in power, imperial majesty, traffic, and riches, but also
in its splendor and virtue and justice, that it is not inferior to any
other place under the sun. Without question, it would take only ten
Venetian merchants to buy all the merchandise that enters the city per
year, along with the city itself.[29] Just to make sure that no one thinks
I say this only to diminish the glory and ambitions of the Spanish
nation, I will give also the same information for Nombre de Dios.

This city [Nombre de Dios] is situated on the Caribbean. Usually
about fourteen or fifteen ships, large and small, arrive every year.
The largest carries 1,800 *salme*.[30] They are filled with diverse things,
mostly wine, wheat, and biscotti. The rest carry oil, some cloth and
silk, and generally just all the kinds of things they have in Spain,
mostly for use in the house, such that sustain human life. Sometimes
it has happened that the market has been so overstocked that the
articles did not fetch the price they originally cost in Spain. I have
seen that they have some goods, like olives, figs, raisins, and other
things that did not sell at any price. They left them with the captain
of the ship for freight. On the other hand, there were times when
there were shortages all around because the ships did not come on
account of fear of the French, and then everything sold, as they say,
for its weight in gold.[31]

29. Comparisons to Old World cities were common. For example, Cortés praised
the Aztecs for governing their territory as well as Venice, Genoa, and Pisa were gov-
erned. See Kim, "Uneasy Reflections"; Keen, *Aztec Image in Western Thought*, 57, 70,
81; Cortés, *Letters from Mexico*, 68.
30. I.e., 360 tons.
31. In 1536, French pirates raided ships off the coasts of Panama and Cuba.
In 1537, they raided more extensively, attacking Cartagena, Nombre de Dios, Havana,
and Santo Domingo.

When the ships arrive at Nombre de Dios, the merchants send the goods in little ships down the Chagres river, to a place called La [Venta de] Cruces, fifteen miles from Panama.[32] There they are given to a Spaniard who holds them until the mule drivers arrive to get them to Panama. Then, in other ships that were built in that sea, most of the goods are sent down to Peru, to all the cities of this large Kingdom of Peru inhabited by Spaniards, including Panama and Nombre de Dios.[33] According to the latest census, the largest population yet is barely 4,000 people. So I think the reader can easily judge whether Panama can be compared in commerce to the richest and most illustrious city of Venice.[34] You find that these Spaniards in this country are so arrogant that they never get tired of praising themselves, especially those who have never been to Italy. Other say that they have taken this fortress and fought on that parapet, that they were always victorious and through their work they conquered and sacked that strong city, and that one Spaniard is worth four Germans, three Frenchmen, and two Italians. They say that without doubt five hundred of them would suffice to take painted Venice, as if she were some village made of twenty-five or thirty straw or wooden houses, like most of the cities they built in the Indies. There are many of them who came from Spain, not only to these Indies but also to all the other provinces they tyrannize, who say in their egotism that they are from Gothic stock—descendants of the Gusmani and Muarichi.[35] Then you learn the truth: in Spain they were pig farmers or shepherds.[36]

32.   This is the first of two routes used to transport merchandise between Nombre de Dios and Panama. The sea route helped lower the cost of transportation but increased the risk by exposing merchants and their cargo to foreign pirates along the coast. Ward, *Imperial Panama*, 56–58.

33.   During much of the sixteenth and seventeenth centuries, Panama served as the primary supply route to and from Peru. Goods traveled from Spain to Nombre de Dios, across the isthmus to Panama City, and then by sea to Lima.

34.   At this time, Venice had well over a hundred thousand residents.

35.   Benzoni is probably referring here to noble houses. The Gusmani probably refers to the de Guzmán family, the dukes of Medina Sidonia.

36.   Farming represented a major sector of the economy of Spain, particularly in the Kingdom of Castile. Much of the wealth of many noble families derived from land rents, taxes, and income generated by livestock, especially sheep. Ruiz, *Spanish Society, 1400–1600*, 42–59, 88.

The city of Panama is situated in a little lowland near the edge of the Southern Sea,[37] near the coast.[38] During the full moon the waves easily reached, or went into, the houses built on that side of town. The other part was surrounded by reeds and by wood, and almost all were roofed with shingles. In my time, the population did not exceed one hundred and twenty houses. The port was good and safe, but small; when the sea rises, ships go in, but when it begins to fall they go out. They can only go partly loaded because the water is shallow and recedes so far that it exposes more than two miles of beach and you can see nothing but mire. The ships stand a bit farther out and load and unload with small boats. The staple articles that are brought to Panama are maize, a little flour from Peru, hens, and honey. They have an abundance of cows, pigs, oranges, lemons, cabbages, onions, lettuces, melons, and other kinds of garden vegetables. This part of Panama used to be the home of many Indian tribes, and all their rivers used to have an abundance of gold. But the Spaniards had consumed everything.

The trip from Panama to Nombre de Dios is fifty miles. The first day the road is good enough, but then it enters a woods and it remains that way until the end. About halfway there is a river that often takes more than three hours to pass.[39] Some Spaniards entered in winter and found themselves in the middle of this river and it began to rain so unrelentingly that it began to rise in such a manner that they had no place to go and drowned. I knew one Spaniard who found himself in this river as it began to swell. There was only one more branch to pass and he was riding a mule carrying gold and jewels worth four thousand ducats. The current carried him down; he attached himself to a branch of a tree and came to shore having lost everything. He arrived in Nombre de Dios wearing only a jacket.

This town is built on the shore, from east to west, in the middle of a great forest. This place is unhealthy, especially in the winter,

37. The Pacific Ocean.
38. Here we have deleted a short passage about a Spanish braggart named Il Montese and his boorish behavior, and eventual embarrassment, in Italy.
39. This is the second route across the isthmus. While safe from pirates, the road passed through treacherous terrain and during the sixteenth century was susceptible to attacks by the runaway slaves who inhabited mountains of the isthmus. Ward, *Imperial Panama*, 58–60.

because of the great heat and the wetness of the earth, and also because of a marsh on the west side. Many men die here. The houses are like those in Panama. When I lived in this territory it was inhabited by fifteen or twenty merchants who sold in bulk. All the other houses and bodegas where inhabited by small merchants, apothecaries, sailors, tavern-keepers, and other useful people. All the merchants who have a house in Nombre de Dios also keep one in Panama and live there until they get rich. On the north shore stands the port, which is big enough for many ships.

In the woods on the eastern side, not too far from Nombre de Dios, there is a population of runaway Moors who have killed many Spaniards sent by the governor to kill them.[40] In these woods near some rivers there are some houses inhabited by Indians, and the Moors have befriended them.[41] They have poisoned arrows, and often they go to the road to Panama and they kill as many Spaniards as fall into their hands, cutting them cruelly to pieces. In winter, because of the contrary winds, the boats that go on the river Chagres take a long time to get to La [Venta de] Cruces. Many times the merchants send certain things to Panama that sometimes fall into the hands of these runaways. They take all the merchandise and leave the Moors who drive the mules alone, unless they want to run away with them.[42] This is the topic of many contracts and treaties between Panama and Nombre de Dios.[43]

It seems to me to be the time to give the entire story of the rotten and cruel country of Veragua, since we are close to it.[44] The reader

40. Throughout the sixteenth century, Maroon communities populated the Isthmus of Panama, and runaway slaves frequently harassed traders and other Europeans. The Spanish organized campaigns of conquest in the 1530s, 1550s, and 1570s. In the 1580s, amnesty was granted to Maroons who surrendered and were resettled in free-black towns. Pike, "Black Rebels"; Tardieu, *Cimarrones de Panamá*.

41. As in other parts of the Americas, Maroons allied with indigenous groups in order to survive in a foreign land and oppose Spanish attempts at reenslavement. For an example from Pacific Colombia, see Beatty-Medina, "Between the Cross and the Sword."

42. Spaniards frequently complained that Maroons captured or recruited slaves working as muleteers. Occasionally, Maroons would even raid Spanish cities to free slaves living there. Such raids continued long after Benzoni's time. Archivo General de Indias (AGI), Panama 30, N. 12, fols. 1–2.

43. Authorities in Panama City and Nombre de Dios had to pay for the defense of the royal roads connecting the two port cities. For example, see AGI, Panama 13, R. 10, N. 29, and Panama 30, N. 12, fols. 1–2.

44. The region known as Veragua included parts of modern-day Panama, Nicaragua, and Costa Rica.

can understand the big difference between speaking of a place one has heard about and speaking from one's own experience.

The fame of this very rich country spread so that a captain was able to interest twenty-seven soldiers in Nombre de Dios.[45] I found myself in that city and wanted to be one of them. I was warned off by an old Spaniard who had traveled for about fifteen years in the provinces of Cartagena and Santa Marta and other places. He told me that I should in no way whatsoever believe the words of the captain, because they will say one thing or another to get what they want.[46] And he warned that even if it was my desire to go, I should at least wait for another trip to see how things went. But I was young, and strong, and full of the spirit of adventure. And I so very much wanted to make myself rich that I didn't want to believe his words. So I determined to go.

And so we went. And at the end of four days we reached the mouth of the Rio Suerre.[47] But it was a big lake and we were not able to enter without great danger, so we turned around and scurried over to the islands of Zorobar,[48] which are near Nuevo Cartago in the province of Veragua. And if this is a bad country, that was worse. These islands are small, and the Indians who used to live there have fled to the mountains on the mainland.

Winter begins in the month of June and the winds are contrary. Because of them, we stayed there for seventy-two days. In that time we did not see four hours of sunshine. Almost constantly, but especially at night, there was an abundance of rain, thunder, and lightning, so much so that it seemed both heaven and earth would be destroyed. A bolt of lightning struck the boat and killed a Moor and two Spaniards. All the rest of us were frightened. The captain landed on the mainland, with the intention of going ashore wherever there were Indians to look for provisions. But after he had walked for eight days and found nothing but woods and swamps, with mountains marvelous to see, he returned along the coast with great difficulty.

45. Here we have omitted a description of Diego Gutierrez's trip to New Spain.

46. Many *adelantados* are likely to have exaggerated the spoils of future conquests in order to recruit more men to their expeditions. The warnings of the jaded old Spaniard reflect the reality that few conquests were as lucrative as advertised.

47. Now known as the Rio Parismina.

48. Possibly the archipelago of San Andrés, Providencia, and Santa Catalina.

He ate only slugs, and some wild fruits that nourished the monkeys, who were always jumping around in the trees.[49]

He led us to the governor.[50] After twenty days the brigantine entered the port and joined us. The governor immediately sent it back to Nombre de Dios for more men. The rest of us rested for some days. In the meantime we caught many giant turtles. For four months they are found in great numbers on the beach because they come to lay their eggs in the earth, like the crocodiles, and the immeasurable heat of the sun hatches them. We skinned them, gathered the fat, melted it down, and put it in clay jars. We salted a little of the meat but it quickly spoiled. But fresh it was very healthy and delicious to eat.

The first day we entered the port, the governor in his graciousness placed me at his table and took pleasure in talking to me. Most of his conversation was about gold, silver, war, and the great cruelties inflicted on poor Italy—especially the city of Milan. But when he figured out that I did not want to hear of such things, he developed a hatred for me and could not even stand to look at me.[51]

After getting provisions, the governor left in his frigate accompanied by four boats of Indians and all of his soldiers. We quickly entered the boundaries of the Suerre about thirty miles upriver. He housed himself in a house owned by a lord of that region that he kept for recreation when he came there to fish.

This house was shaped like an egg, about forty-five paces long and nine paces wide. It was paneled in reeds and covered with braided palm fronds. There were other houses, but they were common. The governor called this town San Francisco, because we arrived on his feast day.[52]

49.   In the original, Benzoni uses the term *gatti mammone*. These magical creatures are common in Italian folktales, a combination of a cat (always depicted as a mystical creature in such folktales) and a demon. He certainly indicates a sort of tree monkey here, but he clearly wants us to understand that it was a terrifying and freakish creature. See Caprettini, *Dizionario della fiaba*, 193–94.

50.   Diego Gutiérrez y Toledo. At the time of his appointment, the region of New Cartago had not been conquered or settled. Gutiérrez was called governor because he had the right to serve as governor after establishing a colony. Molina Castillo, *Veragua*, 65.

51.   Governor Gutiérrez y Toledo probably believed that the Spanish occupation of Milan resulted in "great cruelties."

52.   I.e., October 4, 1544.

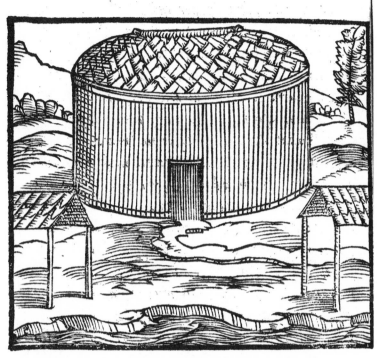

Caſa beniſſimamente coperta
nella prouincia di Suere.

FIG. 8 Well-covered house in the province of Suerre. "Casa benissimamente coperta nella prouincia di Suere." In Benzoni, *La historia del Mondo Nuovo*, 1565. Courtesy of the John Carter Brown Library at Brown University.

We marched five or six days without finding any sort of life at all, through woods and over mountains.[53] Of the latter, we went down one that was more than fifteen miles long. While we were descending, in some places it was so steep that we had to hold on to the roots of trees in order not to fall. Eventually we reached a big, strong river. And there we found some abandoned houses that must have been used by hunters, because inside there were bones and skulls of deer, tiger, and other animals. The governor stayed there for two days,

53. Here we have omitted another story of Spanish cruelty toward some indigenous lords.

where we found a good quantity of mammee apples. Near a small stream we found roots like those found in the island of Hispaniola that they use to make *pan cazabi*.[54] These have a good flavor, so they can be roasted in the coals and cause no harm at all. With these we took care of our hunger. We went on for about three days until we found a crossroads. The governor did not know which one to choose, so he asked an Indian who was with us which was a better way to get to an Indian village. When he responded that he did not know, the governor ordered a few black slaves to kill him. They did, and he said, "This is how we treat bad men." Later he asked the same question of the lord and he also responded the same way: that he did not know. The governor ordered the Moors to do the same to him as they had done to the other. When the lord saw them coming to him, he put down his load and bowed his head, waiting for death with great calm. At this, the governor ordered the slaves to leave him alone and let the lord live.

Three Spaniards, so weary with hunger that they could not stand, stayed here. They were later killed by Indians. That evening the governor, seeing that we had nothing to eat, and not wanting to give us anything, told us to kill the dogs and split the meat among the men. I made a present of my share because it was full of worms. And so I went to the governor with hope that he might give me something but he told me I could go eat the roots of the trees. A Spaniard heard this and said, "My lord governor, since you will not share the good with us as well as the bad, you can go and make war by yourself." Because of those and other words, and the intercession of the captain, the governor grudgingly provided a three-pound piece of cheese to be split in thirty-four parts. And so we passed the evening. The same night our governor ordered the cook to prepare a piece of pork for him and picked me to stand watch until four o'clock in the morning. I stopped by the fire while on patrol and found that everyone was sleeping. Right away I picked up a piece of wood, used my knife to whittle a point on the end, and put it in the cooking pot to pick up a piece of pork. I hid it in my knapsack and immediately returned to guarding, happier than if I had found a great treasure. When the governor learned of it, he was really annoyed, but he said only that

54. *Pan cazabi* was a bread made with yucca flour that was very popular among the conquistadors.

it was time to abandon the cooking pot. Meanwhile, I ate the pork—though it was a bit salty—and left the tree roots there.

After two days we got to the entrance of the woods. We saw an Indian who was watching us from behind a tree. As soon as he discovered us, he leapt off like a deer to warn the lord of the province of our arrival. Over the following days, day and night, a multitude of Indians descended upon us. The governor was answering nature's call near the area from which the enemies arrived and was the first killed. They descended on us with ghastly screams and noises, making a clamor with bells and drums, completely painted red and black, with plumage and golden jewelry at their necks, and with other paraphernalia, as they dress themselves all over the Indies when they go to war.

I wanted to join the battle. I went to get my sword and shield and put a foot in a companion's helmet that was hidden under some leaves. I put that on my head, and by the grace of God, I survived the battle. The Indians shot rocks that dented the helmet in such a way that it looked like a metalsmith had pounded it all over with a hammer. We fought for between a quarter and a half an hour.[55] We wounded and killed many Indians until we made them turn back. But then more reinforcements arrived and a new brawl began. Since the majority of us were tired—more from hunger than from fighting—we were not able to resist the great multitude of furious enemies. We were quickly killed with stones and spears and run through with palm lances. I found myself with the captain. He was hit by a rock thrown from the forest. I saw him fall and I found myself alone. I did not know what to do or where to go. I was frozen with confusion, when two Spaniards came to me, totally covered in blood, saying to me, "What are you doing, Milanese? All of us are already dead. Let's hit the road and head back to where we came from to try to save our lives!" And so I moved on. We passed through a group of twenty-five or more Indians, all of them lords, each one carrying only a single lance and a shield at the shoulder. They were not painted like the others. One threw his lance at my neck but it did me little harm because I had cotton shoved in my doublet.

---

55. Benzoni writes, "per ispatio de mezo quarto d'hora," which translates directly as "for the space of half quarter of an hour." It is unlikely that he means that the battle in which they fought a "multitude" was over in seven and a half minutes. It probably lasted between fifteen and thirty minutes.

We kept going. On the summit of a hill not too far away we found our priest, who had fled from the battle with a couple of soldiers. Within a couple hours we met up with Captain Alonso de Pisa, who arrived with twenty-four Spaniards on the orders of the governor. We were quickly overrun by over 100 Indians with swords, *rotella* shields, and crossbows that they had taken from us. They danced and jumped around, saying in Spanish, "Get gold, Christians! Get gold!" But when they saw how many of us there were, they turned tail and ran.

And so we reached the shore, through great struggle and with great danger. The two Spaniards who were with me at the battle stayed at the foot of the mountain because they were not able to go any further because of their injuries. Then we were joined by two young men who had hidden in the woods when the Indians attacked and stayed there until the Indians had gone away. After they left their hiding place, they found that the Indians had cut off and taken away the head, feet, and hands of the governor and two Moors. They stripped the rest and threw them into the river. Then they carried off everything except the oil and the soap. Among our people, we lost twenty-four Spaniards and two Moors. Six of us survived. Among the enemies, many more died—it is estimated that there were 4,000 of them. It is true that they are very timid. In fact, they are cowardly.

If we had had even four horses we would not have fought at all, because the Indians were terrified of these ferocious animals. It is well known that in battles it is not the valor of the Christians, or the arms, artillery, lances, swords, or crossbows but fear. The fright—the terror—the Indians had of the horses subdued them. And this we know from experience, because in every place where the Spaniards have gone out without horses, they have been conquered by the Indians.[56] And when the Spaniards first arrived in Mexico, the men believed that the men and the horses were one animal.[57]

56.   Like other Spanish conquistadors, Benzoni views horses as a major military advantage, for both the mobility they afforded and their shock value. In 1599, Bernardo de Vargas Machuca listed the horse, harquebus, and war dog as the most fear-inspiring tools of the conquistador. Vargas Machuca, *Milicia y descripción de las Indias*, 159. However, in more confined or difficult terrain (jungles, mountain passes, marshlands, etc.), the advantage of horses may have been considerably smaller. See Restall, *Seven Myths of the Spanish Conquest*, 142.

57.   Although the horse was new to Native Americans, Benzoni is wrong: they did not confuse horse and rider as one creature. In Mexico, Nahuatl speakers created a

Already my readers can understand with what spirit the Spaniards have conquered and dominated these Indian nations. For although they laud themselves in their histories for having always fought for the Christian faith, the experience, especially in these countries, clearly demonstrates that they fought for greed. And this is the truth.

When we reached the shore, we rested there several days because the sea was high.[58] We left when the sea became hospitable via the canal of Nicaragua. We picked up a Portuguese man named Francesco Calato who became a lieutenant because he lent our governor 3,500 gold ducats.[59] Because of contrary winds on the way to Nombre de Dios, we were becalmed for two months. We suffered a great deal because of hunger, and if not for an abundance of crocodile eggs we were able to find on the coast, many of us would have died of hunger.[60] These eggs were as large as goose eggs, and if you pound them on rocks they will dent but not break, so it is necessary to open them with a hammer. The flavor is like half-spoiled moss, and at first I could not eat them at all. But need affects me like everyone else. We also picked up some four-legged animals, called *iguane*, that are shaped like our lizards but with a ridge under their mouths and on the top of their heads that looks a little like that on a rooster and has some points like spines. The females have a light flavor and their eggs have a better flavor than their flesh. They live in the water as much as on the earth.[61]

In the Nicaraguan canal there are many large fish, including a kind that is called *manati* in the language of Hispaniola.[62] I don't know what the Indians who lived there before called them because

---

neologism for the new animals that translates as "people-bearing deer." Wood, *Transcending Conquest*, 49–51.

58. In the original text, Benzoni included a passage here describing other Spanish explorers throughout the New World.

59. Conquistador "ranks" denoted the level of an individual's contribution/investment, not his military experience. There was no lieutenant rank in conquistador companies. Calato may have been named lieutenant governor by Diego Gutiérrez y Toledo, the governor of the province of Nuevo Cartago y Costa Rica.

60. Benzoni uses *vova de cocodrilli*, literally, crocodile eggs. These may have been sea turtle eggs.

61. Beginning in the sixteenth century, observations of new flora and fauna by chroniclers and travelers helped spur new forms of empirical investigation and scientific observation. See Barrera-Osorio, *Experiencing Nature*; Bleichmar et al., *Science in the Spanish and Portuguese Empires*.

62. Manatee, another word of Taíno origin.

they have all gone to the forest to live as a result of bad treatment by the Spaniards. The fish is shaped like an otter.[63] It is twenty-five feet long and eleven feet wide. It has a head and neck like an ox, with small eyes, thick skin, and a dark pelt. It has two feet shaped liked those of an elephant. The females give birth like cows and have two breasts they use to raise their young. I have seen some in the grass in the little islands of this big river. In Nombre de Dios I ate its meat a few times. When salted, its flavor is like pork. Some say that the flavor of this fish is like veal. This I attribute to one of two things: either these Spaniards were so hungry that they thought it had great flavor, or they have never tasted veal.

The customs of the natives of the province of Suerre are much like those already described, except these Indians do not eat the human flesh. Their language is beautiful to learn. They call the earth *ischa*, and men *cici*, illness *stasa*, and gold *chirauchla*.[64] You find huge numbers of wild boars, ferocious tigers, and other, timid, lions. If they see a man, they run away. There are snakes of incredible size but without venom, and apes. There is another animal in this country that is called *cascuij*, shaped like a pig, black and hairy, with a thick skin.[65] The eyes are small but the ears are big, its hooves are split, and like an elephant it has a nose like a trombone. It has a horrendous cry that stuns people. Its meat is flavorful. Another monstrous animal is found that region. It has a pouch under its belly and it puts its young in there when it wants to go from place to place. It has the body and muzzle of a fox, hands and feet like a cat (but they move), and it has ears like a bat.[66] There are also peacocks, pheasants, partridges, and other sorts of birds, all different from ours.

Likewise, there are many bats that fly around at night pecking people, and while they are found all down the coast to the Gulf of Paria, they are not as annoying as they are here. It happened to me in places along this coast, especially in Nombre de Dios, that while I was sleeping, it pecked my toes so delicately that I felt nothing, but in the morning I found the sheets and the mattress so bloody that it seems

63. The word he uses is *ludria*. *Lutra* means otter.
64. These words are from the Talamanca language family.
65. The overall size, shape, color, and nose seem to describe the Central American tapir.
66. This seems to describe a species of opossum, several of which are common to the region.

they gave me a terrible wound.⁶⁷ But in this place they have never bitten me without me noticing, and suffering for two or three hours. Sometimes they would beat their wings around my face. And if I left my socks on they would bite my hands. So I had no other remedy except to always keep some bandages near me when I slept. When I felt them bite, I would immediately bind my wound so I would heal in three or four days.

We left the canal with two other ships that had come from Nicaragua full of provisions. In fifteen days we reached Nombre de Dios. From this city, we sailed 1,000 miles west down uninhabited coast to the province of Fondura.⁶⁸ Three hundred miles farther down on the same coast is the Yucatan. The country is very rocky, but fertile, and there is an abundance of fish, fruits, and corn.⁶⁹ They sacrifice men but they do not eat the flesh. There is no mine of silver or gold of any kind to be found. They raise many bees and grow an abundance of cotton, with which they make capes like sheets and sleeveless shirts. This is the principal tribute they give to their patrons. The Spaniards distribute them in Mexico, the island of Cuba, in the Cape of Fondura, and in other places.

To make a long story short: in the province of Fondura there had been over 400,000 Indians when the Spaniards arrived to conquer. When I visited there were not even 8,000 left. The conquistadors had destroyed them, between those killed in war, sold as slaves, or worked to death in the mines or other unbearable labor. Like the other peoples who serve the Spaniards, these Indians run away to live in some distant place so they can see the Spaniards as little as possible. That is how much love and goodwill they have for them.

The Spaniards built five towns, but between them there are not even 120 houses, and those are built with reeds, covered in straw, and now stand mostly uninhabited since the mines have been nearly exhausted. The largest, Trujillo, on Cabo Vescovado, sits on a little hill on the northern shore. One hundred miles south is Puerto de Caballos.⁷⁰ A day's journey from this port [Puerto de Caballos] lies

67. Probably the common vampire bat. The vampire bat has anticoagulants in its saliva that probably account for Benzoni's excessive bleeding.
68. Honduras.
69. We have omitted a short passage covering the original discovery of the region.
70. Puerto de Caballos (modern-day Puerto Cortés) is roughly a hundred miles to the west of Trujillo. In the colonial period, Puerto de Caballos was one of the major

the town of San Pedro, built on a plain near some mountains and not far from the Rio Ulúa and a lake covered with little islands covered with grass and brush that move around when the wind blows. Eighty miles farther are Comayagua and Gracias a Dios; these two towns are about one hundred miles apart and produce a lot of wheat, as the country is a bit cold. Then we enter into the beautiful, delightful, but already destroyed valley of Olanchio, where the Spaniards erected a town called San Jacobo.[71] This town has about twenty houses, covered in straw and mostly uninhabited.

So that the readers can consider just how well we are seen by the people of these territories, I will tell what happened to me in this valley with some Indians. I left Comayagua with a Spaniard to go to San Jacobo. We went through all of the provisions we carried while walking for four days without seeing even one house. Finally, we reached a small Indian village and we begged the Indians to give us something to eat. But they would not give us anything at all, not for love or money. Instead, they cursed us, spit on the ground with disgust, and told us to go away. That night we reached the town, but there was no inn, so we went to sleep on some reeds in an empty house.

After leaving Fondura and passing the mines of Choluteca, one enters into the province of Nicaragua, which goes all the way to the coast of the Southern Sea.[72] Nicaragua is not very big but it is fertile and delightful, though it is so hot in the summer that people can only go out at night. The soil is sandy. It rains six months of the year, beginning in May, and for the rest of the year it never rains. The night is just like the day. The country produces a lot of honey, wax, balsam, cotton, and many fruits. There is a kind that is not found in Hispaniola, or in other parts of the Indies. It is shaped like our pear but it has a round pit inside about one and half times the size of a walnut. They have a very good flavor. The tree that produces it grows very big and has little leaves. They have very few cows but lots of Spanish pigs. There are many Indian villages, though they are small.

---

ports serving the seat of the Audiencia in Santiago de Guatemala (modern-day Antigua). Herrera, *Natives, Europeans, and Africans*, 24–25.

71. Probably Santiago, San Jacobo in Italian. A city called Santiago in a destroyed valley could refer to the site of Santiago de Guatemala, destroyed in 1541. Yet, later in his account, Benzoni describes Santiago de Guatemala (the passage is not included in this translation) and its destruction, which suggests that this is a different settlement.

72. Several short passages about the Spaniards' behavior have been omitted here.

The houses are made of reeds, covered with straw, and not too big. They have no mines for metals of any sort, but when the Spaniards arrived they had a lot of lesser-alloy gold from other provinces. There are an incredible multitude of parrots that cause a lot of trouble. If the Indians did not frighten them off by throwing stones at them, they would do a great deal more.

The Spaniards named the province Muhammad's Paradise when they first subjugated it because of the great abundance of everything.[73] There are two things produced in this province that you cannot find anywhere else in the Indies except in the territories of Guatemala, the Cape of Fondura, Mexico, and along the shores of New Spain. One is a sort of peacock [that] has been brought back to Europe and is known as an Indian hen.[74] The other is cocoa, which they use as money.[75] It is grown in a medium-sized tree that lives in a warm and shady location. It will die if the sun hits it, so it is planted among the trees in damp woods, but that is not enough. They plant another tree that will grow larger next to it. When it is large enough, they pull down the branches to provide shade so the sun cannot bother the cocoa at all.

The fruit is like an almond and grows in a shell about the size of a pumpkin. It matures in one year. When it is ripe, the seeds are removed and placed in the sun to dry. When they want to drink, they roast the seeds in a pan over the fire, and then they use the stones they use to make bread to grind them. They put this paste in vases (which are like gourds grown in a certain tree that is found in every part of the Indies) and add warm water bit by bit. Sometimes they add a bit of their pepper. They drink it but it seems to be more of a drink for pigs than men.[76]

73. Although this claim would be repeated by later authors, its origin is unclear. In the seventeenth century, Thomas Gage, an English traveler, writer, and clergyman, also called the region by this name. Gage, *English-American*, 75.

74. The peacock discussed here is probably a turkey. Oviedo discusses them similarly, calling them *galline della India*, as do other contemporary sources. See Eiche, *Presenting the Turkey*, chap. 2.

75. In central Mexico and much of Central America, cocoa beans, cotton blankets, and gold dust were used as mediums of exchange. Hassig, *Trade, Tribute, and Transportation*, 67–69.

76. Indigenous hot chocolate was bitter and sometimes spicy; many Europeans found it unpalatable until sugar became a common and inexpensive sweetener. Schivelbusch, *Tastes of Paradise*, 85–94. Marcy Norton argues in "Tasting Empire" that the

Albero che produce il cacauate, & come gl'Indiani di due legni cauano fuoco.

cacauate

FIG. 9 Trees that produce cacauate [cacao, or cocoa] and how Indians make fire with two sticks. "Albero che produce il cacauate, & come gl'Indiani di due legni cauano fuoco." In Benzoni, *La historia del Mondo Nuovo,* 1565. Courtesy of the John Carter Brown Library at Brown University.

I was in that country for more than one year without ever tasting that beverage. When I went through villages, Indians would offer me the beverage and laughed in amazement when I refused. But, since there was no wine and I didn't want to drink only water all the time, I came around. Its flavor is slightly bitter, but it sates you and refreshes the body without intoxicating. This is the best and most

---

ubiquity of chocolate in Mesoamerica, coupled with sustained social and cultural contact between indigenous groups and Spaniards, eventually led some Spaniards to gain an appreciation for the drink despite its foreign flavor profile.

Alberi che producono le zucche, del che gl'Indiani generalmente fe ne feruano de' uafi.

FIG. 10 Trees that produce gourds the Indians use as vases. "Alberi che producono le zucche, del che gl'Indiani generalmente se ne seruano de' uasi." In Benzoni, *La historia del Mondo Nuovo*, 1565. Courtesy of the John Carter Brown Library at Brown University.

expensive thing they have and the Indians value it most of all. Their customs are all almost like those of the Mexicans:[77] They eat human flesh and wear sleeveless tunics and cloaks. They make fire with two sticks as they do in all of the Indies. They have lots of wax but they don't know what to do with it, so they use wood of wild pine to make a torch. They speak four languages, but the best is Mexican, which is spoken in more than 1,500 miles of country and is the easiest to

77. Benzoni's use of "Mexicans" here refers to the practices of the Mexica (Aztecs) of central Mexico.

Modo di ballare.

FIG. 11 How to dance. "Modo di ballare." In Benzoni, *La historia del Mondo Nuovo*, 1565. Courtesy of the John Carter Brown Library at Brown University.

learn.[78] They call men *tutruane*, bread *tascal*, and hens *totoli*, and *occomaia* means wait a minute, and sickness *mococova*, and dancing *mitote*. This is how they dance.

Two or three hundred, or even three or four thousand, depending on the province, gather together. They clean the square where they want to dance. One of them goes forward to lead the dance. He almost always goes backward, turning around several times, as do all the others, three or four in a line. The drummers begin to sing

78.   Although some Nahuatl speakers settled Central America as allies of the Spanish during the conquest era, Benzoni is probably describing the closely related language of Pipil. Matthew and Romero, "Nahuatl and Pipil in Colonial Guatemala."

some of their songs and the man who leads the dance is the first to respond. All the rest do the same, hand in hand. Some carry a fan, some a maraca of gourd with pebbles inside. Some wear plumage on their heads, others wear lines of seashells on their arms and on their legs. Some turn in one way, some in the other, some raise their legs, some wave their arms around. Some pretend to be blind and some act as if they were crippled.[79] They laugh and they cry. Doing these things and other things and drinking from their glasses, they dance all day and sometimes part of the night.[80]

End of the Second Book

---

79. For an examination of indigenous dance and its representation and misrepresentation by early colonial observers, see Scolieri, *Dancing the New World.*

80. The rest of Book II involves a story about a greedy monk seeking gold and secondhand accounts of other conquests.

Book III

The ships leave Panama to go to Peru, generally from the month of January until the end of April.[1] That is the best time of all the year because these are the summer months and the Greek and Levante winds usually blow.[2] Those who leave in other times have considerable troubles. After the ships are loaded, they leave Panama and go to Tobago and other islands in the area to pick up fresh water. These islands are called the Pearls because the Spanish found a lot of those there.[3] Then they navigate about 100 or 150 miles west. They do this because there is a strong current that continually runs east. After that, they cross to Peru. When I sailed from Panama to get to Peru, it was in the month of June. That is wintertime and most of the passengers got sick because of the winds.[4] Because the ships that travel in this sea do not have sheltered accommodations like the ships in the North Sea, the passengers have to stay out in the rain. This is how we reached Gorgona Island.[5]

When the master of the vessel saw this island, he said, "This is the devil's land," because it is the worst possible way to get to those territories. Some have said that it never quits raining, but they are wrong. It is true that it rains eight months of the year so unrelentingly, with

1. We have omitted a good deal about Pizarro and the conquest of Panama from the beginning of Book III.

2. Benzoni is referring to winds from the east and northeast.

3. The Pearl Islands are located off the Pacific coastline southwest of Panama City.

4. Benzoni views the rainy season as winter. Although Panama is near the equator, it is still in the Northern Hemisphere and would be experiencing summer in June.

5. Francisco Pizarro stayed on Gorgona Island for seven months in 1527, after a failed expedition down the coast. Prescott, *History of the Conquest of Peru*, 1:264.

FIG. 12 How the Indians live in the trees. "Come gli Indiani viuono sopra gli Arbori." In Benzoni, *La historia del Mondo Nuovo*, 1565. Courtesy of the John Carter Brown Library at Brown University.

thunder and lightning, that it seems that the elements are fighting one another. When we arrived it was already spring, which begins at the end of May. That is how it is: when winter begins in Panama, the spring starts here.

Along the coast of this island, the inhabitants had much gold and have their houses in the tops of trees. Because this land is so swampy, the horses can't cross it, and the Spaniards have never been able to conquer it. One summer, Gaspar de Andagoya[6] was in the Bay of San

6.   Benzoni has conflated Pascual de Andagoya with someone else, possibly Gaspar de Espinosa, another conquistador active in this region. See Clements Markham's introduction in Andagoya, *Proceedings of Pedrarias Davila*, xx–xxii.

Mateo with 150 soldiers and went raiding throughout the province.[7] Sometimes they used boards as shields because whenever possible the Indians would defend themselves with rocks, lances, jugs of boiling water, and many other things. Then the Spaniards would use good axes to cut down the trees and everything would fall to the earth with a loud crash. Many times the Indians maimed or killed some of the Spaniards. But because the country is so difficult and cannot sustain many men, Andagoya took a huge quantity of gold and left it, and no Spaniards live there any longer.

All of the ships that travel on this coast for most of the year suffer inopportune winds from the west and south. Also, because of the strong current they have to anchor on the beach every evening and in the morning raise anchor and sail with the island wind. Sometimes they plan to go forward but instead drop backward and stay put for fifteen or twenty days in the same place. This is what happened to us. And so we found ourselves in sight of Cabo San Francisco, 130 miles from Cabo de Paseo, which is at the end of Cabo Viejo.[8] We thought the place was inhabited by Indians, as it had been before. But all of us passengers were out of provisions because it had already been three months since we left Panama. We saw that the merchants on board would rather leave us to die of hunger rather than give us a scrap of bread, so we decided to go ahead by land. Twenty-four of us departed on this venture, each carrying four little containers of corn.[9] We crossed at the four rivers of Quisime, one after the other, with great difficulty and danger, by strapping together some trees we found on the beach.

The water is salty, and because of the strong flow of the sea the salt runs more than fifteen miles inland in the rivers. Because of that, when we wanted to drink it was necessary to dig wells. When we reached Cabo de Paseo we found that the Indians had burned their houses and had gone into the woods. We went through to the

7. Benzoni's geography is unclear. In 1540, Pascual de Andagoya undertook a campaign of conquest near the Rio San Juan (in present-day Colombia). The Bay of San Mateo is significantly farther south, near Manta, Ecuador. Andagoya's campaign on the Rio San Juan encroached on the neighboring Spanish conquests of Sebastián de Belalcázar, which would ultimately lead to Andagoya's arrest. Ibid., xxvi–xviii.

8. These are various capes between Colombia and Peru.

9. Europeans preferred wheat to corn. That they carried corn on this voyage rather than wheat indicates that no wheat was available in Panama, or that it was too expensive.

other part of the cape and arrived at the Gulf of Caráquez. This gulf lies south of the equator. We didn't know where to go, or how to get across to the other part. Having nothing better to eat, we ate crabs that had so little meat on them we also ate the bones, and a few yellow berries, and some fresh water from a little lake that we found in the woods near the shore. And so we lived for twenty-two days until the ship came into port. They were sure that we all had starved to death or that the Indians had killed us. When the captain saw us, he immediately sent the boat, and we rested on the boat that night. The next day we left for Portoviejo.[10]

This city is inhabited by Spaniards; they have twenty-two reed houses thatched with straw. This province is just about destroyed and ruined. The natives have many emeralds and they still hold the mines. However much the Spaniards have tormented them, and killed many, they still did not want to tell where they were. I heard from a majordomo of Captain Juan de Olmos that his Indian concubine told him where it was but that he did not want to reveal the location for fear that the king would take it from him.[11] They also had a similarly large number of vases of gold and silver but the Spaniards took everything, and so right now they can only give their masters what they can pick up in the province. Because of this, only a few Spaniards live there.

Some say that the Indians of this province have abandoned the bad customs and deceptions of their false religion and that their false gods have stopped their responses because they have heard the words of the Holy Gospel from the priests and the monks. But what I can say to this is: God wish it were so. I can testify with surety that there were never priests or monks who moved among those people to preach to them or to teach them our faith. The Indians publicly laughed at them and said that they did not want to be Christians, because of our wickedness. And even though President de la Gasca commanded that there should be priests and monks in every village to teach the doctrine to the children, the Spaniards of this town, like others before them, appealed.[12] They argued that a priest would want

10. Portoviejo was founded in 1535 and is located ninety miles north-northwest of Guayaquil.

11. A *mayordomo* typically managed estates of wealthy Spaniards, often overseeing their laborers. Lockhart, *Spanish Peru*, 23–25.

12. Pedro de La Gasca served as president of the Audiencia of Lima and as interim viceroy (1546–49). The New Laws of 1542 required that *encomenderos* pay clergy to

400 ducats a year for salary and that all the Indians combined did not give that in tribute to their lords.[13] But since I left Peru about this time, I do not know what came of this.

While I was in this province, every now and then to pass the time I would go to the Indian villages, both inland and on the coast. One day in a little village called Charapoto, I found the Indians in the temple making their sacrifices.[14] Hearing them playing their drums and singing some of their songs, I wanted to see. I went inside the temple, but immediately the priest saw me. He chased me out angrily, almost spitting in my face. I saw a clay idol in the shape of a tiger and two peacocks, and other birds that they kept for sacrificing to their gods. They might have had a little boy, as is their custom, but I did not see him. Another day I went to Picalanceme and found the Indians of this village drinking. I wanted to stay and see how they got drunk, but four of them came up to where I was standing, and told me in Spanish, "Oh, you villainous Christian, get out of our country!" They came at me so I grabbed my sword and got away. I decided not to go to the villages anymore on their feast days.

I also went to other towns, like Cama, Camuliova, Camuxiova, and other places.[15] In some of them, the Indians kill their children so they won't have to serve the Spaniards. It is said for certain that the lords of Manta have an emerald the size of a chicken egg that they revere as their principal deity. This city of Manta is situated on the shore and it was one of the main cities of this coast. Before the Spaniards arrived in their country, there were more than 2,000 Indians. But at the present you will find only about fifty, just like in all the other villages of this province. One day López de Ayala asked the lord of this city if he wanted to be Christian, and he responded that he did not know but that he (de Ayala) could do what he liked. And so the lord was baptized and named Don Diego. But despite all this I never

preach in their *encomiendas*. Spaniards tended to ignore this requirement, which in turn led royal officials to reiterate the requirement frequently. Schwaller, *Catholic Church in Latin America*, 81.

13. Four hundred ducats were worth about 500 pesos *de oro común*, an exorbitant salary for a rural clergyman. In central Mexico, salaries for rural parish priests ranged between 250 and 300 pesos *de oro común*. Schwaller, *Origins of Church Wealth*, 8.

14. The pueblo of Charapoto is located about ten miles north of Portoviejo.

15. These towns are in the region surrounding Portoviejo. For a more in-depth description of the various ethnic groups of coastal Ecuador, see Newson, *Life and Death*, 61–78.

saw him look a Spaniard in the face. His vassals were ugly, dirty sod-
omites full of every sort of evil.

Usually, the people who live on this coast drink fresh water by
digging large wells, and when they go to other places they carry a
gourd full of water. When the Indians of Manta go to Portoviejo,
they do not like to carry water from their wells, fearing that they will
meet the Spaniards who will drink it. Instead, they go two miles over
land to get black, dirty, stinky water that comes from a rock, because
they are sure the Spaniards will not drink it.

This country is hot and humid and you never see a quiet sky.
There are many deer, pigs, and Spanish hens, and here they make the
best bread out of maize that you will find in all of the Indies. Some
say that it is better than wheat bread, but I do not want to agree to
such a thing. They make a good deal of honey but it is sour and waxy,
and not very good. They also produce a sort of fruit like figs that the
natives call papaya, some large and some small, of a sort I have never
seen in other provinces, only in this place. The tree is tall and delicate
and the fruit is of a sweet taste. There is also another sort of small fig,
full of spines, called *tuna*,[16] but this you can find in other countries
like Nicaragua and Guatemala, and all over the Kingdom of New
Spain.

Generally all the Indians of the province of Portoviejo get a certain disease called *berugue*.[17] It attacks the face and other parts of
the body. Most of the boils are the size of a walnut, and I've had my
share. They don't hurt at all but they are ugly and bloody. There is no
cure for them, except to let them mature and then cut them delicately
with some thread. These people dye their faces, and they pierce their
noses and lips, and ears, and cheeks, and when they have their festivals they put jewelry in them. Most of them wear their usual dress—
a tunic without sleeves—others go completely nude and sometimes
they dye their entire bodies black.

All along this coast, the Indians are great fishermen. The boats
they use to fish and to sail are a kind of raft made of three, five,
seven, nine, or eleven very thin timbers lashed together in the shape
of a hand. The center is longer than the ends; some are long and some

16. Cactus fruit, from the Spanish *tuna*.
17. Probably from *verruga*, Spanish for wart. It is unclear what disease Benzoni is
describing.

Il modo di pescare, & nauigare nel mare di Mezzo giorno.

FIG. 13 How to fish and sail in the Mezzogiorno sea. "Il modo di pescare, & nauigare nel mare di Mezzo giorno." In Benzoni, *La historia del Mondo Nuovo*, 1565. Courtesy of the John Carter Brown Library at Brown University.

short, with sails of corresponding size. The Indians have space to row. When they are becalmed and too tired to row any longer the Indians throw bread, fruit, and other things in the water, like a sacrifice, praying that they can bring a good wind.

Past the ends of Portoviejo you enter the country of Guancavelica, a smaller province in the Kingdom of Peru.[18] The first hamlet you find on the coast is called Colonche, which sits in the area at the point

18. Not to be confused with the mercury mines in southern Peru called Huancavelica. This "country of Guancavelica" was inhabited by an indigenous group of that name.

of Santa Elena. I saw the lord of that tribe many times. He could have been about sixty years old, and he really had the air of a lord. He had a robust and extremely healthy body. He went about in a tunic without sleeves, dyed red, and at his neck he wore a necklace of six doubloons of finest gold, in the style of a big coral. On his hand he wore a ring, and similarly had pierced ears full of jewels and gold, and on his left arm near his hand he wore a certain shiny stone like a mirror, to keep his sight.[19] These people remove five or six of their upper teeth, and if you ask them why, they will say it is for beauty's sake. They wear a little sleeveless tunic, like they do in Portoviejo. They cover their shameful parts with a band of cotton that hangs down to the earth in the back like the tail of a horse. The women wear a cloth cinched like a belt that falls down to the middle of the legs.

The people of this province serve the Spaniards who live in the city of Guayaquil. This city they first built on the banks of the Chiono river, about forty miles from the seashore.[20] In that area there are certain marvelous and frightful plains, a great country full of water and thick woods, and an incredible quantity of crocodiles. And besides this, eight months of the year there are so many mosquitos that I have wondered how the Spaniards could stand to live there. When the Spaniards go to bed at night they have to put themselves under a tent. The Indians do the same thing, but theirs are up high, on top of four huge stilts with a little sunroof, and they sleep like this so the mosquitos cannot annoy them as much.

In the year '46, because of the huge amount of rain, the river was so engorged that it not only destroyed the city, but also the surrounding country.[21] Because of this, the Spaniards moved twenty miles down, near the shore, and built on the bank of this river, called the Huayna Cápac Crossing.[22] It had that name because Huayna Cápac sent one of his captains with a good number of men to conquer the province. He ordered the peasants to build a bridge to cross the

19. Here we have omitted a passage about a former lord of the territory.

20. The river Benzoni mentions may be the Rio Chone, but there is some debate over the original location of the city of Guayaquil. Other early sources do not mention the Chiono; Benzoni's geography may be confused. Gómez Iturralde, *Crónicas, relatos y estampas*, 1:15–18.

21. The city was relocated several times for various reasons during the 1530s and 1540s. Ibid., 18–24.

22. Benzoni calls it the Guainacava Crossing. It seems to be named after the last pre-Hispanic Inca leader, Huayna Cápac. Moseley, *Incas and Their Ancestors*, 10.

river out of large logs in the same way they would make a raft. And as the people began to cross it, their enemies broke the bridge by cutting the ropes. Many of Huayna Cápac's people drowned and the logs fell on the rest, killing almost everyone. Huayna Cápac heard about the massacre of his people. He left Quito with a large army and, descending from the mountains, attacked the Indians and massacred them. Then he wanted to build a road across the river by throwing in earth and stones to safely cross from one side to the other. So he started work on this major undertaking, but after having gone about twenty feet in, he found the rivers so strong and powerful that he gave up on his plan. This is why the Spaniards call this Huayna Cápac Crossing, but the town is called Santiago [de Guayaquil]. Like the others around it, looks like Portoviejo.

Puná Island, which belongs to the king, sits at the mouth of the river.[23] The people of this island, as well as the denizens of the riverbanks, have always warred with the Spaniards as long as they had the strength, and have killed many of them. Among others: Fray Vicente de Valverde and forty-two other Spaniards rested here after escaping the fury of Don Diego when he killed Marques Francisco Pizarro. At night the Indians beat them with sticks, killing them all.[24]

In Puná, and in the territories of Guayaquil and Portoviejo, there is a certain root, with many branches shaped like oaks, called *Zarzaparilia*, that cures the French disease and many other infirmities.[25] To give it to a sick person, it is ground finely between two sticks to extract the juice. That is mixed with a little hot water. The patient drinks until he can drink no more, then stays in a warm place and sweats as much as possible. They stay like this for three or four days, more or less, eating

---

23. That this island "belongs to the king" means that there was no *encomendero*; the tribute and labor of the indigenous residents were paid to the king instead.

24. Between 1537 and 1542, Spaniards in Peru fought a long civil war over control of the region. Francisco Pizarro and his brothers led one faction, while the other was led by Diego de Almagro, whom Pizarro killed in 1538. The war was rekindled shortly thereafter, and in 1541 Diego de Almagro the Younger killed Pizarro. Andrien, *Andean Worlds*, 41–45.

25. The "French disease," syphilis, originated in the New World. It was probably carried back to Europe by Columbus's men. In 1495, an outbreak among French troops fighting in the Italian Wars led to its nickname, the "French disease." Meyer et al., "Syphilis 2001." By the end of the sixteenth century, *sarsaparilla* had been adopted by European physicians as a treatment for various illnesses, including syphilis. Huguet-Termes, "New World Materia Medica," 368–72.

only biscuits and a bit of roasted fowl. Some boil its twigs in water to drink during the day for two or three more months.

In the province of Guayaquil, and other areas further east, the winter begins in the month of November and lasts until April. Spring begins in May and ends in October. Sometimes, along the southern shore, starting at Tumbes, so little rain falls for three or four years that the inhabitants must augment the heavy night dew with irrigation during the day in order to grow crops. There are certain regions where it never rains. In the mountains it rains eight months of the year and many of those areas are always covered in snow and ice. In summer, certain winds blow constantly from the south that bother the residents very much.

When I left Guayaquil to go to Quito, I passed the mountain of Chimino, which is more than forty miles high and completely uninhabited.[26] If not for the succor of an Indian who gave me some water, I would have died of thirst on the road. I found myself on the summit, just standing for a while looking around, considering this strange and marvelous country. I seemed to see things that both existed and did not, as if it were a vision.

In the great province of Quito as in other parts of Peru, although many people had their own languages, the Inca mandated that everyone learn the language of Cuzco, and that the fathers teach it to their children. Thus, they generally use this language in all the territories they rule.[27]

These people continue to speak with demons, holding the sun as their principal god. When they want to ask for certain favors, the lords or the priests ascend a high rock at sunrise with bowed heads, and clap their hands, rubbing them, then raising them in a strange way as if they wished to touch the sun. They say certain prayers and ask for what they needed. So at present, when the Spaniards treat them badly, they worship them as if they were the sun, begging that they show them mercy and not do them any harm.[28]

26. Probably the volcano Chimborazo. Benzoni's claim of forty miles probably refers to the length of the road traversing the mountain's peak rather than its vertical height.

27. I.e., Cusco Quechua. The imperial languages of Nahuatl and Quechua were spoken widely in their respective regions both before and after the Spanish conquest. See Andrien, *Andean Worlds*, 117; and the essays in Schwaller, "Language of Empire."

28. Missionaries often struggled to extirpate everyday rituals and devotions. Mills, *Idolatry and Its Enemies*.

Come gl'Indiani del Peru adorano il Sole, & lo tengono per il ſuo principal Iddio.

FIG. 14 How the Indians of Peru worship the sun and keep it as their primary god. "Come gl'Indiani del Peru adorano il Sole, & lo tengono per il suo principal Iddio." In Benzoni, *La historia del Mondo Nuovo*, 1565. Courtesy of the John Carter Brown Library at Brown University.

The temples, especially those of the sun, are big and sumptuous, and the interior walls were decorated with plates of gold and silver. They have many virgins called *mamacone*, who spin and weave only for their god. They sacrifice men and children but they don't eat the meat. They sacrifice sheep, birds, and other animals in the same way and wipe the blood on the faces of the idol at the door of the temple. When they want to communicate with a demon or plant, or really to begin any venture, the priests fast for several days. When a lord dies, they build a great tomb and they bury him with much gold and worked silver and with some of his most beautiful and dear wives and servants. They also put in some clothing, grain, wine, and things to eat and drink, enough to sustain them until they arrive in the other world. This manner of burial is used in many parts of the Indies. They believe in the immortality of the soul. The Spaniards have found many very rich graves, though very few compared to those that are still there. They mourn for their dead for many days.[29]

The men dress in a sleeveless tunic of silk or cotton and a cape gathered together on one shoulder. The nobles encircle their heads with a headscarf and wear a woolen bow that hangs down to their ear on the left. They make shoes out of a white herb like hemp. The women wear a long cloak that covers them from the shoulder down to the feet. They cinch that with a sash four fingers wide that they call a *chumbi*. On their neck they wear certain long pins of gold and silver called *topi*.[30] On top they wear another little cape called a *liquida*.[31] They wear long hair. And this is the manner of dress in all of Cuzco.

When they go out for a walk they rub a certain red paste on their face because of the wind. They carry an herb called coca in their mouths and this must provide some sort of sustenance because they can walk all day without eating or drinking anything.[32] This herb is their principal cash crop. They have roots, called *papa*, kind of like truffles, but with little flavor.[33] They used to have a lot of sheep, as big as asses, almost like camels, but they say that not too long ago a disease like leprosy hit, and a great number of them died.[34] But that was not as bad as the leprosy, that is, the Spaniards, who destroyed almost everything. The meat of this animal is gamey. The natives used to wear the wool of these animals but now there is a great shortage. The great joy for these people, as in many provinces, is to drink. When they are good and drunk, each of them takes a woman who looks best and enflames their lust, barely thinking about their mothers and children. The lords marry their sisters.

29. Benzoni's summary of Inca religion is quite superficial and is geared toward emphasizing eccentric practices. For a more detailed description of Inca religion, see Hyland, *Gods of the Andes*.

30. Probably the Quechua word *tipki*, meaning needle.

31. The name for this garment seems to derive from a Spanish-Castilian root, not from Quechua.

32. Coca leaves, the source of cocaine, have a stimulating effect and can suppress appetite. Malpass, *Daily Life in the Inca Empire*, 8, 83.

33. The Quechua word for potato. At the time of the conquest, there were hundreds of varieties of potato under cultivation in the region. Ibid., 82–83.

34. This description refers to llamas or vicuñas, South American camelids.

They do not make bread of any kind; rather, they eat all their grain either boiled or roasted. This was one of the rules Huayna Cápac laid down. When he wanted to run off on some enterprise, he did not want his people to be busy making bread. And so they still observe this law.

The principal city of this kingdom used to be Cuzco, the head of the Incan Empire.[35] According to the natives, it was built a long time ago by Manco Cápac, the first king of that lineage.[36] After that, his descendants added so much to their territory by subjugating many different peoples, and they gave them their laws and customs.[37] In every place they have built many large buildings, both to serve their gods and also in service of the king. These buildings' walls were made of a soft stone called pumice in Italy, and they are all thatched with straw. I have seen them all over these parts but especially in the province of Quito, in the territory of Tumebamba.[38] All are as sumptuous as those in Cuzco. The Spaniards have destroyed a great many of them, but a good number still exist along the roads, and they are called by the people *tambi*. You can still see the fabric of these grand buildings.

Huayna Cápac built a very good road descending from the hills to the plain. This province of Quito has a temperate climate, and because of this the king of Cuzco lived there most of the time. He employed many goldsmiths there who, though they did not have any iron instruments, still made wonderful things. They worked like this:

First thing, to melt gold or silver, put it in either an oblong or round jeweler's crucible made of cloth smeared with dirt and charcoal dust. After that dries, it is put into the fire filled with metal. Five or six men, sometimes more, sometimes less, with cannon-shaped reeds, blow on it until it melts. Then it is pushed out of the crucible. The goldsmiths sit on the ground and with certain black rocks fashioned for this purpose help one another make—or, more correctly, used to

---

35. The term Inca (or Incan) Empire takes its name from the title of its ruler, the "Inca." The Quechua name for the empire was Tawantinsuyu.

36. Manco Cápac is the mythical progenitor of the city-state of Cuzco, which would ultimately expand the territory under its control and become the Inca Empire. Malpass, *Daily Life in the Inca Empire*, 102–3.

37. The major expansion of the Inca Empire began under the leadership of the Pachacuti Inca Yupanqui (r. 1438–71). Ibid., xxv–xxvii.

38. Tumebamba was a regional administrative capital in the northern part of the Inca Empire.

Il modo che tengono gli orefici
nel lauorare, & fondere
l'oro,&l'argento.

FIG. 15 How goldsmiths work and mix gold and silver. "Il modo che tengono gli orefici nel lauorare, & fondere l'oro, & l'argento." In Benzoni, *La historia del Mondo Nuovo*, 1565. Courtesy of the John Carter Brown Library at Brown University.

make when they were prosperous—whatever they are asked to make, for instance hollow statues, cases, sheep, jewelry, and, finally any animals they saw.

As for Spanish products, a great deal of wheat is found in all the cold and temperate locations of this kingdom. There are also some vines but little fruit. Some say that they hope that they will be able to make wine in this country very soon and they grow most of the fruits of Spain. But by my judgment, although you can't crush hopes, these will never be realized, because the air and the constellation of the seasons are in every way contrary to ours. And, moreover, in other places in New Spain better than Peru, they have not managed to grow grapes. They will not here.[39] I also say that the goodness of God would not give liquor to these brutes and only gives them the things necessary to sustain their life. The Spaniards have an abundance of radishes, lettuce, melons, cucumbers, cabbages, and some figs. They do not have an abundance of lemons and oranges, because these fruit only grow in hot climates. They have few cattle as a result of the constant war.[40] When I was in Lima, a cow was worth 120 gold ducats and a sheep between fifty and sixty. Quito is the most fertile and abundant province in Peru, yielding a lot of wheat and supporting many pigs and Spanish roosters. Besides that, a huge number of tasty rabbits can be found continually.

Wine is really expensive, and in the city of Quito, when there is a good sale, a cask of wine that holds twelve jugs and weighs twenty-eight ounces, more or less, costs fourteen or fifteen gold ducats. In Lima, and other locations, that is, on the coast, it costs ten or twelve ducats. But in Potosí, which is more than 500 miles inland, the price is seventy or eighty ducats. It varies like this in every place, according to the country where it is carried.[41] Because the jugs or bottles the wine is carried in are made of earth and brought from Spain and carried from one place to the other, many are broken. Sometimes because of the tardiness of the ships, there is such a shortage that people pay 400, or 500, or even 1,000 gold ducats for one jug.

Now, it seems to me to be time to tell the false opinions these people have of us. After the Spaniards entered Peru, the Indians saw how they comported themselves and the great cruelties they committed in every area. Not only would they never believe that we are Christians and the sons of God, as the Spaniards had told them, but not even that we were people born on this earth. They say that it is not possible that we are born of man and woman together, but that

39. Although the colonial wine industry did develop very slowly, modern-day Chile, once the southernmost part of the Inca Empire, boasts a very prosperous winemaking industry.

40. This comment alludes to the regional devastation caused by the Pizarro-Almagro civil war of the 1530s and '40s.

41. The topography of the Andes made transportation very difficult. All goods had to be carried by humans or pack animals. Malpass, *Daily Life in the Inca Empire*, 69.

we are fierce animals born of the sea. So they call us *viracochas*.[42]
In their language the word for sea is *cocha* and the foam *vira*, and so
they say that the sea congealed and the froth nourished us and so we
have come onto the earth to destroy the world, and other things that
even omnipotent God himself could not correct in their mind.[43] They
say that the wind destroys houses and knocks over trees but these
viracochas devour everything, consuming the earth, give froth to
the rivers, and never rest, always hurrying from one part to another.
They seek gold and silver but they are never satisfied, gambling it
away, warring, robbing, swearing, and acting like renegades.[44] They
never speak the truth, and they have taken away our sustenance.
Finally, they curse the sea for placing such vicious and wicked people
on the earth. Going around the various parts of the kingdom, I often
met Indians, and to amuse myself, I would ask them where to find a
certain Christian and they would not acknowledge me in any way.
They would not even look me in the face. But if I asked where to find
a *viracocha* they would respond right away. When the children can
barely say a word, their father would show them one of us and they
would say, "Look! A *viracocha*!" But many tribes of this kingdom,
being rich, have priests and friars to teach them and instruct the children with the gospel.[45] God willing, their efforts will bring fruit.

I have already told you about the abundance of riches that the
Spaniards found in this kingdom when they first conquered it.[46] But
after all of this, the Indians pick up a huge bowl of maize and take
from it one grain, saying, "this the *viracochas* have taken away, but
the rest remains in the country." In order that these riches would not
fall into the hands of the Spaniards, they have thrown it into the sea
and buried it in the ground. The Spaniards have found many large
and rich mines, both of gold and of silver. The richest that they have

42.   Viracocha was the creator deity of the Inca pantheon. Ibid., 103–4. Chroniclers
and conquistadors often repeated the claim that natives viewed Spaniards as gods.
Modern scholars believe that such claims tell us more about the Spanish mindset of
the time than about any indigenous belief. See Gose, *Invaders as Ancestors*, 3–7.

43.   *Viracocha* translates as "sea foam."

44.   Aztec accounts also describe Spaniards as monkeys squabbling over gold.
Restall, Sousa, and Terraciano, *Mesoamerican Voices*, 29.

45.   In other words, they have a priest because the community has the wealth to
pay his salary.

46.   Here we have omitted a story about a Flemish monk who attempted to found
a monastery in Quito.

discovered are the silver mines at Potosí, and they found gold in a river called the Calvaia[47] near Cuzco. Also in the province of Quito there is another very rich river called Santa Barbara, and finally, they have also found it in some mountains. In these places they dig deep under the ground, and hold up the tunnels with huge beams until they have dug everything out. Sometimes everything collapses, killing everyone inside, Spaniards and slaves alike.[48] The gold they get from these mountains is like the finest sand, and it is separated from the earth using quicksilver.[49] That which comes from the river comes in both large and small grains. Right now, the gold mines are almost all dry. They still mine silver but not in the quantity they used to. If we always take away and never restore, no mountain is so large that it will not end.

The cities the Spaniards have built in this Kingdom of Peru are Lima, Arequipa, Cuzco, Ciudad Nuevo, Villa de la Plata, Trujillo, Huanuco, Chachapoyas, Quito, San Miguel, and Portoviejo. The largest is Lima; it has 450 hearths. The others have twenty, thirty, forty, fifty, and eighty houses. Finally, I conclude that if all the cities that the Spaniards have built in these Indies, which they say amount to 300, were added together, you could find that there are fewer people than in the town of Porta Comasina of Milan. Because in its prime this town was able to send out 12,000, not including its elders. In these days, you cannot find more than 14,000 or 15,000 people, including young and old.

Three years after I arrived in Peru, I found myself in possession of several thousand ducats and fed up with these territories. President de la Gasca had ordered all the foreigners to leave Peru because some Spaniards had told him those from the east, that is, us, that we were false and cruel and the cause of the death of many Spaniards.[50]

47. Probably the Carabaya River.
48. Most labor in Andean mines came from natives mobilized through the *mita*. This labor draft predated the Spanish and was used extensively by the Incas to help build and maintain public works. Andrien, *Andean Worlds*, 24–25, 61–62.
49. Mercury was used to extract silver from low-grade ore by creating a silver-mercury amalgam. Brown, *Mining in Latin America*, 19.
50. Many non-Iberians participated in the early exploration and conquest of the Americas. Lockhart, *Spanish Peru*, 114–34. Over time, the presence of these foreigners came to be problematic. European wars, such as the Italian Wars, brought natives of those regions under suspicion. Foreign merchants threatened New World profits. In 1523, the Spanish Crown prohibited foreign merchants from working in the

So I found myself in the city of Guayaquil, boarding a boat full of merchandise from Panama, and I decided to leave and come to my country. On the order of the captain, we embarked on the 8th of May, 1550. In the port of Salango, we found President de la Gasca, who was going to Panama in order to make the crossing to Spain. He ordered our captain to sail with him because otherwise he would have to go alone. But because we had to load maize, our captain asked if we could stay to see to our needs. The president left and we stayed in port until the ship was full. We left and quickly reached Manta. There the boat hit a rock and sank.[51] All the passengers and sailors and most of their gold and silver were saved. This happened because we did not have a good pilot, because the other, who had guided the ship from Panama, had stayed in Guayaquil because of a royal order from Spain that had arrived all over the Indies regarding married men. At the request of the married women of Spain, presidents and governors had to either send their married men back to Spain or to bring over their wives.[52] Our pilot was scared that because he had no powerful friends he would be sent back to Spain, and he did not want to return. So he stayed in Peru.

Because the boat was wrecked, as I said, I had to wait for another passage. At the end of fifty days a ship arrived from Lima and we quickly sailed for Panama. Having heard that the president had left Nombre de Dios for the trip to Spain with all the ships, I went to Nicaragua.[53] There I endured a long and very grave illness, so much so that at the end of four years I found myself still in Guatemala.[54] When the ships arrived from Spain I went to the Puerto de Caballos, and I got on a ship. We left, and having sailed for several days, we found ourselves near the island of Cuba when we were hit by a

---

Americas (Archivo General de Indias, Indiferente 420, L. 9, fol. 170v), and in 1535, authorities on Hispaniola received orders to identify and deport foreigners, excluding Portuguese men (AGI, Indiferente 422, L. 16, fol. 228r–v).

51. Salango and Manta are only about fifty miles apart by sea.

52. Most conquistadors did not earn enough from the spoils of conquest to return to Spain in the manner they had hoped. Many continued to try and get rich in the Americas while their wives and children lived on in Spain. To avoid these long separations, the king ordered that married men return to Spain or send for their wives (AGI, Indiferente 421, L. 11, fols. 193v–194r).

53. Ships typically traveled in convoys to protect themselves from pirates. Lane, *Pillaging the Empire*, 18.

54. Nicaragua was a province within the Audiencia of Guatemala.

huge storm that drove us to the coast. Almost all of the cargo was lost; the crew was barely saved.

After thirty-four days of danger and hard work we reached Havana, expecting to see the armada. Unfortunately, we found that they had left eight days before on the route to Spain, with Diego Gaytano as the captain. Midway through the passage they encountered a terrible storm. Out of eighteen vessels, thirteen were lost in the gulf. In one was Clavisso,[55] governor of Panama, and two judges from the new Kingdom of Granada, who were being taken to Spain in chains by order of the king for their robbery and injustice. Two others arrived in Santo Domingo torn to pieces. The other three made the passage to Spain. One went ashore on the coast of Portugal but some of her passengers were saved. The other arrived in Cadiz. The admiral's ship was wrecked near Sanlúcar de Barrameda and about 200 people drowned. The captain saved himself, along with some of his crew and his concubine, and arrived in Seville, and shortly after he was incarcerated at the command of the king, accused of causing all of the trouble by leaving the Indies at such a time that it would mean reaching the coast of Spain in winter, when it was most dangerous. He tried to claim innocence, saying that he had to leave Havana because they could not find provisions to sustain so many men, and other things, and eventually he was given his freedom but was deprived of his office.

I found myself in Havana, miserable for two reasons: one because I had lost part of my small fortune on the above-mentioned ship, and also because I learned that the fleet had left. But on hearing of the new and terrible wrecks, I praised God and his divine grace that he saved me and did not let me embark on that ship, otherwise I would certainly have died with the others. Ten months later the fleet of the Indies arrived in Havana, consisting of fourteen ships, big and small, and we quickly left with the help of God. At the end of 39 days, and after enduring a cruel storm, we arrived at a Portuguese island called Madeira. This island is, according to the cosmographers, more than 4,000 miles from Havana. Halfway along the course of the voyage there is a small island called Bermuda. But we did not see it—and similarly few sailors have seen it. And so in Madeira we took on bread and wine and other provisions and then again set sail. After

---

55. Probably Sancho de Clavijo, governor of Panama from 1550 to 1553.

eight days, on the 13th of September, 1556, we entered Sanlúcar de Barrameda, and then on to Seville. As soon as I could I went on to Cadiz, then got on a hulk, and after two months I reached Genoa, where I rejoiced heartily, and soon after arrived in Milan. I always praised the majesty and power of God, the Savior, who granted me grace to see so many new things, and so much of the world, and so many strange countries, and saved me from innumerable difficulties. When I think about it, it seems almost impossible that a human body could endure so much.

Selected Editions of *The History of the New World*

Benzoni, Girolamo. *La historia del Mondo Nuovo.* Venice: Appresso Francesco Rampazetto, 1565.

———. *La historia del Mondo Nuovo.* 2nd ed. Venice: Ad instantia di Piero & Francesco Tini, Fratelli, 1572. Reprint, Graz: Akademische Druck- u. Verlagsanstalt, 1962.

———. *La historia del Mondo Nuovo.* Venice: G. Giolito de Ferrari, 1575.

———. *Novae Novi orbis historiae.* Translated by Urban Chauveton. Geneva: Eustathium Vignon, 1578. Reissued in 1581.

———. *Histoire nouvelle du Nouveau Monde.* Translated by Urban Chauveton. Geneva: Par Eustace Vignon, 1579.

———. *Der Newenn Weldt und indianischen Königreichs: newe unnd wahrhaffte History.* . . . Translated by Nicholas Höniger. Basel: Gertruckt durch Sebastian Henric Petri, 1579.

———. *De Historie van de nieuwe weerelt.* . . . Translated by Carel van Mander. Haarlem: Paeschier van Wesbus, 1610.

———. *Quadriga salutis. Or the four general heads of Christian religion surveyed and explained, 1. First, in aphorisms or positive maxims. 2. Secondly, resolved into Questions and answers: With some few annotations annexed at the latter end.* London: By Sarah Griffin, for Philip Chetwind, 1657.

———. *Scheeps-togt na West-Indien, van Hieronymus Benzo.* . . . Leiden: Pieter van der Aa, 1706.

———. *History of the New World by Girolamo Benzoni, Shewing His Travels in America from AD 1541 to 1556, with Some Particulars of the Island of Canary.* . . . Works Issued by the Hakluyt Society 21. London: Hakluyt Society, 1857.

———. *Il primo viaggio intorno al globo di Antonio Pigafetta e le sue Regole sull'arte del navigare; Girolamo Benzoni e la sua Historia del Mondo Nuovo.* Racolta di documenti e studi, pt. 5, vol. 3. Rome: Ministero della Pubblica Istruzione, 1894.

———. *La historia del Mundo Nuevo.* Caracas: Academia Nacional de la Historia, 1967.

————. *La historia del Mundo Nuevo de Jeronimo Benzoni, Milanes*. Lima: Universidad de San Marcos, 1967.

de Bry, Theodor. *Conquistadores, Azteken en Inca's: Gravures*. Amsterdam: Van Hoeve, 1596.

Other Primary Sources

Andagoya, Pascual de. *Narrative of the Proceedings of Pedrarias Dávila in the Provinces of Tierra Firme or Castilla del Oro: And of the Discovery of the South Sea and the Coasts of Peru and Nicaragua*. Translated and edited by Clements R. Markham. London: Hakluyt Society, 1865.

Cortés, Hernán. *Cartas de relación*. Edited by Angel Delgado Gómez. Madrid: Editorial Castalia, 1993.

————. *Letters from Mexico*. Translated and edited by Anthony Pagden. New Haven: Yale University Press, 1986.

Eannes de Azurara, Gomes. *Cronica do descobrimento e conquista de Guiné*. Ca. 1450. Paris: J. P. Aillaud, 1841.

Francis, J. Michael. *Invading Colombia: Spanish Accounts of the Gonzalo Jiménez de Quesada Expedition of Conquest*. Latin American Originals 1. University Park: Pennsylvania State University Press, 2007.

Gage, Thomas. *The English-American, his travail by sea and land, or, a New survey of the West-India's. . . .* London: R. Cotes, 1648.

Hyland, Sabine. *Gods of the Andes: An Early Jesuit Account of Inca Religion and Andean Christianity*. Latin American Originals 6. University Park: Pennsylvania State University Press, 2011.

Las Casas, Bartolomé de. *History of the Indies*. Translated and edited by Andrée Collard. New York: Harper & Row, 1971.

————. *In Defense of the Indians: The Defense of the Most Reverend Lord, Don Fray Bartolomé de Las Casas, of the Order of Preachers, Late Bishop of Chiapa, Against the Persecutors and Slanderers of the Peoples of the New World Discovered Across the Seas*. Translated by Stafford Poole. DeKalb: Northern Illinois University Press, 1992.

————. *A Short Account of the Destruction of the Indies*. Edited and translated by Nigel Griffin. London: Penguin Books, 1992.

Lockhart, James, and Enrique Otte, eds. *Letters and People of the Spanish Indies: Sixteenth Century*. Cambridge: Cambridge University Press, 1976.

Polo, Marco. *The Travels of Marco Polo, the Venetian*. New ed. New York: Everyman's Library, 2008.

Purchas, Samuel. *Hakluyts Posthumus or Purchas his Pilgrimes, containing a History of the World in Sea Voyages and Lande Travells, by Englishmen and Others*. 4 vols. London: Featherstone, 1625.

Restall, Matthew, and Florine G. L. Asselbergs. *Invading Guatemala: Spanish, Nahua, and Maya Accounts of the Conquest Wars*. Latin

American Originals 2. University Park: Pennsylvania State University
   Press, 2007.
Restall, Matthew, Lisa Sousa, and Kevin Terraciano, eds. *Mesoamerican Voices:
   Native-Language Writings from Colonial Mexico, Oaxaca, Yucatan,
   and Guatemala*. Cambridge: Cambridge University Press, 2005.
Schwaller, John Frederick, with Helen Nader. *The First Letter from New
   Spain: The Lost Petition of Cortés and His Company, June 20, 1519*.
   Austin: University of Texas Press, 2014.
Schwartz, Stuart B., ed. *Victors and Vanquished: Spanish and Nahua Views
   of the Conquest of Mexico*. Boston: Bedford/St. Martin's, 2000.
Vargas Machuca, Bernardo de. *Milicia y descripción de las Indias*. 1599.
   Madrid: Librería de Victoriano Suarez, 1892.
Whitehead, Neil L. *Of Cannibals and Kings: Primal Anthropology in the
   Americas*. Latin American Originals 7. University Park: Pennsylvania
   State University Press, 2011.

Secondary Sources

Allegri, Marco. *Di Girolamo Benzoni e la sua Historia del Mondo Nuovo*.
   Rome: Ministero della Pubblica Istruzione, 1894.
Altman, Ida. "The Revolt of Enriquillo and the Historiography of Early
   Spanish America." *Americas* 63, no. 4 (2007): 587–614.
Andrien, Kenneth J. *Andean Worlds: Indigenous History, Culture, and Con-
   sciousness Under Spanish Rule, 1532–1825*. Albuquerque: University
   of New Mexico Press, 2001.
Arranz Márquez, Luis. *Don Diego Colón, almirante, virrey y gobernador de
   las Indias*. Vol. 1. Madrid: Consejo Superior de Investigaciones Cientí-
   ficas, Instituto "Gonzalo Fernández de Oviedo," 1982.
Arrom, José Juan. "Cimarrón: Apuntes sobre sus primeras documentaciones
   y su probable origen." *Revista española de antropología americana* 13
   (1983): 47–57.
Barrera-Osorio, Antonio. *Experiencing Nature: The Spanish American
   Empire and the Early Scientific Revolution*. Austin: University of
   Texas Press, 2006.
Beatty-Medina, Charles. "Between the Cross and the Sword: Religious Con-
   quest and Maroon Legitimacy in Colonial Esmeraldas." In *Africans
   to Spanish America: Expanding the Diaspora*, edited by Sherwin K.
   Bryant, Rachel Sarah O'Toole, and Ben Vinson III, 95–113. Urbana:
   University of Illinois Press, 2012.
Benzoni, Maria Matilde. *La cultura italiana e il Messico: Storia di un'immagine
   da Temistitan all'Indipendenza (1519–1821)*. Milan: Unicopli, 2004.
Bleichmar, Daniela, Paula de Vos, Kristin Huffine, and Kevin Sheehan, eds.
   Science in the Spanish and Portuguese Empires, 1500–1800. Stanford:
   Stanford University Press, 2008.

Brown, Kendall W. *A History of Mining in Latin America: From the Colonial Era to the Present.* Albuquerque: University of New Mexico Press, 2012.

Campbell, Mary B. *The Witness and the Other World: Exotic European Travel Writing, 400–1600.* Ithaca: Cornell University Press, 1988.

Caprettini, Gian Paolo, ed. *Dizionario della fiaba: Simboli, personaggi, storie delle fiabe regionali italiane.* Rome: Meltemi Editore, 1998.

Caraci, Ilaria Luzzana, ed. *Scopritori e viaggiatori del Cinquecento e del Seicento.* Vol. 1, *Il Cinquecento.* Milan: Riccardo Ricciardi Editore, 1991.

Cook, Noble David. *Born to Die: Disease and New World Conquest, 1492–1650.* Cambridge: Cambridge University Press, 1998.

Crosby, Alfred W. *The Columbian Exchange: Biological and Cultural Consequences of 1492.* Thirtieth anniversary ed. Westport, Conn.: Praeger, 2003.

Davis, Ralph. *The Rise of the Atlantic Economies.* Ithaca: Cornell University Press, 1973.

del Castillo Mathieu, Nicolas. *Descubrimiento y conquista de Colombia.* Bogotá: Banco de la República, 1988.

Eiche, Sabine. *Presenting the Turkey: The Fabulous Story of a Flamboyant and Fabulous Bird.* Florence: Centro Di, 2004.

Enders, Angela, and Elisabeth Fraser. "An Italian in the New World: Girolamo Benzoni's 'Historia del Mondo Nuovo.'" *Dispositio* 17, nos. 42–43 (1992): 21–35.

Faggi, Paola. "Rileggendo Benzoni, osservatore nelle Indie nuove." *Richerche storiche* 36, no. 3 (1996): 545–63.

Fisher, John R. *The Economic Aspects of Spanish Imperialism in America, 1492–1810.* Liverpool: Liverpool University Press, 1997.

Gamboa Mendoza, Jorge Augusto. *El cacicazgo muisca en los años posteriores a la Conquista: Del sihipkua al cacique colonial (1537–1575).* Bogotá: Instituto Colombiano de Antropología e Historia, 2010.

Gibson, Charles. *The Aztecs Under Spanish Rule: A History of the Indians of the Valley of Mexico, 1519–1810.* Stanford: Stanford University Press, 1964.

———, ed. *The Black Legend: Anti-Spanish Attitudes in the Old World and the New.* New York: Knopf, 1971.

Gómez Iturralde, José Antonio. *Crónicas, relatos y estampas de Guayaquil.* Vol. 1, *1534–1820.* Guayaquil: Talleres Gráficos del Archivo Histórico de Guayas, 2005.

Góngora, Mario. *El estado en el derecho indiano: Época de fundación (1492–1570).* Santiago: Instituto de Investigaciones Historio-Culturales, Facultad de Filosofía y Educación, Universidad de Chile, 1951.

Gose, Peter. *Invaders as Ancestors: On the Intercultural Making and Unmaking of Spanish Colonialism in the Andes.* Toronto: University of Toronto Press, 2008.

Gray, Lewis Cecil. *History of Agriculture in the Southern United States to 1860.* 2 vols. Washington, D.C.: Carnegie Institution of Washington, 1933.

Greenblatt, Stephen. *Marvelous Possessions: The Wonder of the New World.* Chicago: University of Chicago Press, 1992.

Guillot, Carlos F. *Negros rebeldes y negros cimarrones: Perfil afroamericano en la historia del Nuevo Mundo durante el siglo XVI.* Buenos Aires: Librería y Editorial "El Ateneo," 1961.

Hadfield, Andrew. *Amazons, Savages, and Machiavels: Travel and Colonial Writing in English, 1550–1630; An Anthology.* Oxford: Oxford University Press, 2001.

Hanke, Lewis. *All Mankind Is One: A Study of the Disputation Between Bartolomé de Las Casas and Juan Ginés de Sepúlveda in 1550 on the Intellectual and Religious Capacity of the American Indians.* DeKalb: Northern Illinois University Press, 1974.

———. "A Modest Proposal for a Moratorium on Grand Generalizations: Some Thoughts on the Black Legend." *Hispanic American Historical Review* 51, no. 1 (1971): 112–27.

Hassig, Ross. *Mexico and the Spanish Conquest.* 2nd ed. Norman: University of Oklahoma Press, 2006.

———. *Trade, Tribute, and Transportation: The Sixteenth-Century Political Economy of the Valley of Mexico.* Norman: University of Oklahoma Press, 1985.

Herrera, Robinson A. *Natives, Europeans, and Africans in Sixteenth-Century Santiago de Guatemala.* Austin: University of Texas Press, 2003.

Higman, B. W. *A Concise History of the Caribbean.* New York: Cambridge University Press, 2011.

Huguet-Termes, Teresa. "New World Materia Medica in Spanish Renaissance Medicine: From Scholarly Reception to Practical Impact." *Medical History* 45, no. 3 (2001): 359–76.

Humbert, Jules. *Historia de Colombia y de Venezuela.* Translated by Roberto Gabaldón. Caracas: Academia Nacional de la Historia, 1985.

Izard, Miguel. *Tierra firme: Historia de Venezuela y Colombia.* Madrid: Alianza Editorial, 1987.

Jones, Ann Rosalind. "Ethnographer's Sketch, Sensational Engraving, Full-Length Portrait: Print Genres for Spanish America in Girolamo Benzoni, the De Brys, and Cesare Vecellio." *Journal of Medieval and Early Modern Studies* 41, no. 1 (2011): 137–71.

Kamen, Henry. *Spain, 1469–1714: A Society of Conflict.* 4th ed. London: Routledge, 2014.

Keen, Benjamin. *The Aztec Image in Western Thought.* New Brunswick: Rutgers University Press, 1971.

———. "The Black Legend Revisited: Assumptions and Realities." *Hispanic American Historical Review* 49, no. 4 (1969): 703–19.

———. "The Legacy of Bartolomé de Las Casas." In Keen, *Essays in the Intellectual History of Colonial Latin America*, 57–69. Boulder: Westview Press, 1998.

Kellogg, Susan. *Law and the Transformation of Aztec Culture, 1500–1700.* Norman: University of Oklahoma Press, 1995.

Kim, David Y. "Uneasy Reflections: Images of Venice and Tenochtitlan in Benedetto Bordone's 'Isolario.'" *RES: Anthropology and Aesthetics* 49–50 (Spring–Autumn 2006): 80–91.

Kuznesof, Elizabeth A. "Ethnic and Gender Influences on 'Spanish' Creole Society in Colonial Spanish America." *Colonial Latin American Review* 4, no. 1 (1995): 153–76.

Lane, Kris E. *Colour of Paradise: The Emerald in the Age of Gunpowder Empires.* New Haven: Yale University Press, 2010.

———. *Pillaging the Empire: Piracy in the Americas, 1500–1750.* Armonk, N.Y.: M. E. Sharpe, 1998.

Lévi-Strauss, Claude. *Tristes tropiques.* New York: Penguin, 1992.

Lockhart, James. *The Nahuas After the Conquest: A Social and Cultural History of the Indians of Central Mexico, Sixteenth Through Eighteenth Centuries.* Stanford: Stanford University Press, 1992.

———. *Spanish Peru, 1532–1560: A Colonial Society.* Madison: University of Wisconsin Press, 1968.

Mallett, Michael Edward, and Christine Shaw. *The Italian Wars, 1494–1559: War, State, and Society in Early Modern Europe.* Harlow, UK: Pearson, 2012.

Malpass, Michael Andrew. *Daily Life in the Inca Empire.* Westport, Conn.: Greenwood Press, 1996.

Maltby, William S. *The Black Legend in England: The Development of Anti-Spanish Sentiment, 1558–1660.* Durham: Duke University Press, 1971.

Mancall, Peter. "The Age of Discovery." *Reviews in American History* 26, no. 1 (1998): 26–53.

Martinengo, Alessandro. *Il giudizio di Girolamo Benzoni su Las Casas: Denigrazione e censura.* Bern: Franke, 1978.

Martínez, María Elena. "The Black Blood of New Spain: Limpieza de Sangre, Racial Violence, and Gendered Power in Early Colonial Mexico." *William and Mary Quarterly* 61, no. 3 (2004): 479–520.

Martin-Fragachan, Gustavo. "Intellectual, Artistic, and Ideological Aspects of Cultures in the New World." In *General History of the Caribbean*, vol. 2, *New Societies: The Caribbean in the Long Sixteenth Century,* edited by P. C. Emmer, 247–307. London: Macmillan, 1999.

Matthew, Laura E., and Michel R. Oudijk, eds. *Indian Conquistadors: Indigenous Allies in the Conquest of Mesoamerica.* Norman: University of Oklahoma Press, 2007.

Matthew, Laura E., and Sergio F. Romero. "Nahuatl and Pipil in Colonial Guatemala: A Central American Counterpoint." In "A Language of Empire, a Quotidian Tongue: The Uses of Nahuatl in Colonial

Mexico," ed. Robert C. Schwaller, special issue, *Ethnohistory* 59, no. 4 (2012): 765–83.

Mena García, María del Carmen. *La sociedad de Panamá en el siglo XVI.* Seville: Excma. Diputación Provincial de Sevilla, 1984.

Meyer, C., C. Jung, T. Kohl, A. Poenicke, A. Poppe, and K. W. Alt. "Syphilis 2001—A Palaeopathological Reappraisal." *HOMO—Journal of Comparative Human Biology* 53, no. 1 (2002): 39–58.

Mills, Kenneth. *Idolatry and Its Enemies: Colonial Andean Religion and Extirpation, 1640–1750.* Princeton: Princeton University Press, 1997.

Molina Castillo, Mario José. *Veragua: La tierra de Colón y Urracá.* Panama City: Arte Gráfico Impresores, 2008.

Moore, Jerry D. *Architecture and Power in the Ancient Andes: The Archaeology of Public Buildings.* Cambridge: Cambridge University Press, 1996.

Morgan, Jennifer L. "'Some Could Suckle over Their Shoulder': Male Travelers, Female Bodies, and the Gendering of Racial Ideology, 1500–1770." *William and Mary Quarterly* 54, no. 1 (1997): 167–92.

Moseley, Michael Edward. *The Incas and Their Ancestors: The Archaeology of Peru.* London: Thames & Hudson, 1992.

Newson, Linda A. *Life and Death in Early Colonial Ecuador.* Norman: University of Oklahoma Press, 1995.

Norton, Marcy. "Tasting Empire: Chocolate and the European Internalization of Mesoamerican Aesthetics." *American Historical Review* 111, no. 3 (2006): 660–91.

Ortona, Egidio, ed. *Le Americhe: Storie di viaggiatore.* Milan: Nuovo Banco Ambrosiano/Electra Editrice, 1987.

Owensby, Brian P. *Empire of Law and Indian Justice in Colonial Mexico.* Stanford: Stanford University Press, 2008.

Partridge, William, "Cannabis and Cultural Groups in a Columbian Municipio." In *Cannabis and Culture,* edited by Vera Rubin, 147–72. The Hague: Mouton, 1975.

Payne, Anthony. "From the 'History of Travayle' to the History of Travel Collections: The Rise of an Early Modern Genre." In *Richard Hakluyt and Travel Writing in Early Modern Europe,* edited by Daniel Carey and Claire Jowitt, 25–44. London: Hakluyt Society; Burlington, Vt.: Ashgate, 2012.

Peabody, Sue. *There Are No Slaves in France: The Political Culture of Race and Slavery in the Ancien Régime.* New York: Oxford University Press, 1996.

Perocco, Daria. *Viaggiare e raccontare: Narrazione di viaggio ed esperienze di racconto tra Cinque e Seicento.* Alessandria: Edizione dell'Orso, 1997.

Pike, Ruth. "Black Rebels: The Cimarrons of Sixteenth-Century Panama." *Americas* 64, no. 2 (2007): 243–66.

Powell, Philip Wayne. *Tree of Hate: Propaganda and Prejudices Affecting United States Relations with the Hispanic World.* New York: Basic Books, 1971.

Prescott, William H. *History of the Conquest of Peru.* Vol. 1. Edition Deluxe of the Complete Works of William H. Prescott. Philadelphia: J. B. Lippincott, 1874.

Restall, Matthew. *Seven Myths of the Spanish Conquest.* New York: Oxford University Press, 2003.

Romeo, Rosario. *Le scoperte americane nella coscienza italiana del Cinquecento.* Rome: Editori Laterza, 1989.

Rosselli, Ferdinando. *La "Historia del Mondo Nuovo" de Girolamo Benzoni milanese: Contrasti e polemiche su una cronaca italiana del XVI secolo.* Florence: Universitá degli Studii, 1979.

———. "Voci ispaniche ne *La historia del Mondo Nuovo* di Girolamo Benzoni." *Studi dell'Istituto Linguistico* 2 (1979): 3–38.

Ruiz, Teofilo F. *Spanish Society, 1400–1600.* Harlow, UK: Longman, 2001.

Sanders, William T., Alba Guadalupe Mastache, and Robert Cobean, eds. *El urbanismo en Mesoamérica.* Vol. 1. University Park: Pennsylvania State University; Mexico City: Instituto Nacional de Antropología, 2003.

Sauer, Carl Ortwin. *The Early Spanish Main.* Berkeley: University of California Press, 1966.

Schivelbusch, Wolfgang. *Tastes of Paradise: A Social History of Spices, Stimulants, and Intoxicants.* New York: Vintage Books, 1993.

Schwaller, John Frederick. *The History of the Catholic Church in Latin America: From Conquest to Revolution and Beyond.* New York: New York University Press, 2011.

———. *Origins of Church Wealth in Mexico: Ecclesiastical Revenues and Church Finances, 1523–1600.* Albuquerque: University of New Mexico Press, 1985.

Schwaller, Robert C., ed. "A Language of Empire, a Quotidian Tongue: The Uses of Nahuatl in Colonial Mexico." Special issue, *Ethnohistory* 59, no. 4 (2012).

Scolieri, Paul A. *Dancing the New World: Aztecs, Spaniards, and the Choreography of Conquest.* Austin: University of Texas Press, 2013.

Sued-Badillo, Jalil. "The Indigenous Societies at the Time of the Conquest." In *General History of the Caribbean,* vol. 1, *Autochthonous Societies,* edited by Jalil Sued-Badillo, 259–91. London: UNESCO and Macmillan, 1999.

Tardieu, Jean-Pierre. *Cimarrones de Panamá: La forja de una identidad afroamericana en el siglo XVI.* Madrid: Iberoamericana Editorial, 2009.

Thornton, John K. *Africa and Africans in the Making of the Atlantic World, 1400–1800.* 2nd ed. Cambridge: Cambridge University Press, 1998.

Trimborn, Hermann. "La organización del poder público en las culturas soberanas de los chibchas." In *Muiscas: Representaciones, cartografías y etnopolíticas de la memoria,* edited by Ana María Gómez Londoño, 298–314. Bogotá: Editorial Pontificia Universidad Javeriana, 2005.

Villa-Flores, Javier. "'To Lose One's Soul': Blasphemy and Slavery in New Spain, 1596–1669." *Hispanic American Historical Review* 82, no. 3 (2002): 435–68.

Ward, Christopher. *Imperial Panama: Commerce and Conflict in Isthmian America, 1550–1800*. Albuquerque: University of New Mexico Press, 1993.

Warf, Barney. "High Points: An Historical Geography of Cannabis." *Geographical Review* 104, no. 4 (2014): 414–38.

Whitehead, Neil L. *Lords of the Tiger Spirit: A History of the Caribs in Colonial Venezuela and Guyana, 1498–1820*. Dordrecht: Foris, 1988.

———. "The Snake Warriors: Sons of the Tiger's Teeth; A Descriptive Analysis of Carib Warfare, ca. 1500–1820." In *The Anthropology of War*, edited by Jonathan Haas, 146–70. Cambridge: Cambridge University Press, 1990.

———. "South America/Amazonia: The Forest of Marvels." In *The Cambridge Companion to Travel Writing*, edited by Peter Hume and Tim Youngs, 122–38. Cambridge: Cambridge University Press, 2002.

Whitfield, Peter. *Travel: A Literary History*. Chicago: University of Chicago Press, 2011.

Winter, Joseph C., ed. *Tobacco Use by Native North Americans: Sacred Smoke and Silent Killer*. Norman: University of Oklahoma Press, 2000.

Wood, Stephanie Gail. *Transcending Conquest: Nahua Views of Spanish Colonial Mexico*. Norman: University of Oklahoma Press, 2003.

Zavala, Silvio A. *Las instituciones jurídicas en la conquista de América*. 2nd ed. Mexico City: Editorial Porrúa, 1971.

latin american originals

Titles in Print